Satisfaction of Interest and the Concept of Morality

Satisfaction of Interest and the Concept of Morality

Steven A. Smith

Lewisburg: Bucknell University Press
London: Associated University Presses

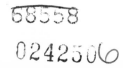

Associated University Presses, Inc.
Cranbury, New Jersey 08512

Associated University Presses
108 New Bond Street
London W1Y OQX, England

Library of Congress Cataloging in Publication Data

Smith, Steven A   1939-
   Satisfaction of interest and the concept of morality.

   Bibliography: p.
   1. Ethics. I. Title.
BJ1012.S52   170   73-8305
ISBN 0-8387-1383-1

To Daryl and David

Contents

Preface

This book addresses itself to a question that has received increasing attention from moral philosophers in recent years. Loosely (and somewhat misleadingly) put, the question is the following: How is morality to be properly defined? Humans guide their behavior by a variety of systems of normative principles and attitudes; and among the various systems of action-guiding principles and attitudes to which an individual or a group adheres, there is usually found something that may be termed a morality—as opposed, for instance, to a code of etiquette or aesthetics. Setting aside for the moment the question of what is morally right or wrong, good or bad, and concentrating upon morality *per se,* we may ask how the moral may be distinguished from the nonmoral. Hence the question: How is morality to be properly defined?

One point made above deserves especial emphasis: my concern is *not* with *normative* questions of morality. I do not seek to determine the *proper* principles of moral conduct, the most *desirable* moral ideals, the *appropriate* principles of justice, or anything of the sort. I inquire, instead, into the logical limits of what can count as a morality *simpliciter,* whether that morality be attractive or unattractive, primitive or enlightened, acceptable or unacceptable. Hence my inquiry is to be sharply distinguished from projects such as John Rawl's recent, and extremely impressive, *A Theory of Justice,*[1] which is obviously, among other things, a treatise in normative moral theory. Unjust moral schemes (whether unjust by Rawls's account, or by some other account) are moral schemes nevertheless.

This study divides naturally into two parts. The first part, comprised by chapters 1, 2, and 3, addresses itself rather generally to the nature of morality amid its diverse manifestations. This first part seeks to explore the concept of morality and to lay down some provisional parameters for any satisfactory analysis, but it stops considerably short of a complete definition. The first three chapters thus attempt to state a kind of prolegomena to any satisfactory analysis of the concept of morality. Chapters 4 and 5, on the other hand, are largely negative in import: they examine and reject a number of closely related accounts of what something must be in order to count as a morality. The accounts that are rejected hold that for anything to count as a morality, it must in some way provide for the satisfaction of human interests and the harmonization of interpersonal conflicts. While these accounts are ultimately rejected, I believe that the examination and discussion of them casts considerable light upon the concept of morality itself. Nevertheless, at the end of the study the basic question—how is morality to be properly defined?—remains an open one. What I hope to have achieved is not a complete analysis of the concept of morality, but a) a very provisional and partial delimitation of that concept, and b) a refutation of several related popular definitions.

1. (Cambridge, Mass.: The Belknap Press of Harvard University Press, 1971).

Acknowledgments

I am indebted to numerous individuals for assistance in the preparation of this book. Special thanks are due to Thomas E. Hill, Jr., and to Charles King for helpful comments on the substance of the study, to Harriet King for excellent typing services, and to Mathilde E. Finch of Associated University Presses for her careful editing of copy. But my greatest debt is owed to Professor Roderick Firth and Professor Robert Nozick, both of Harvard University, whose extensive advice enabled me to avoid many significant defects in the book, and who contributed freely and helpfully of their own views on the substance of the book. Those many defects which remain are, of course, my own responsibility.

I also wish to thank the following publishers for permission to quote from copyrighted material:

Harvard University Press, for permission to quote from John Ladd, *The Structure of a Moral Code,* 1957.

Macmillan Publishing Co., Inc., for permission to quote from the *International Encyclopedia of the Social Sciences,* Vol. 10, article by Lawrence Kohlberg, "Moral Development"; Vol. 12, article by Henry W. Brosin, "Obsessive-Compulsive Disorders"; Vol. 13, article by Hervey M. Cleckley, "Psychopathic Personality"; copyright 1968.

The Press of Case Western Reserve University, for permission to quote from May Edel and Abraham Edel, *Anthropology and Ethics: The Quest for Moral Understanding.* Reprinted by permission from

Satisfaction of Interest and the Concept of Morality

1
Introduction

The Objective

The purpose of the following inquiry is to investigate the notion of a morality. What is a morality? By what criteria may it be recognized? In a very general way, these questions may be readily answered: a morality is a set of beliefs or attitudes about what things are good or bad, right or wrong, praiseworthy or blameworthy—and perhaps a set of dispositions or inclinations to act in some way upon those beliefs or attitudes, given appropriate circumstances. But such a definition is not only overly broad; it is also so vague as to be of little value. And any attempt to make it more precise encounters considerable resistance. In the first place, the phenomenon of morality is immensely complex, subtle, and varied. Hence any attempt to clarify the meaning of the term *morality,* if it is to be faithful to its subject matter, must attempt to accommodate to some degree this complexity, subtlety, and variation. In the second place (and of even more immediate concern to us), the very sense of the question "What is morality?" is not itself clear. Before we can begin to look for an answer to the question, the question must be clarified to some degree. I will begin this clarification by indicating some of the sorts of things that I am *not* attempting to do.

My enterprise is not an exercise in what is commonly called "normative ethics." I do not aim to establish any answers to questions about what things are actually good, right, or praiseworthy (or the respective contraries of these qualities). Nor do I aim to give a detailed conceptual analysis of any one, specific moral term such as *duty, responsible,* and the like as that term is used in English. Furthermore I am not, except peripherally, concerned with "moral epistemology," that is, with how moral claims are *properly* defended, and the extent (if any) to which genuine moral "knowledge" is possible. These remarks sharply distinguish my enterprise from the chief concerns of most major moral philosophers, from Plato and Aristotle down through the history of moral theory to contemporary moral philosophers such as John Rawls and others.

What then is the nature of this inquiry? It can be partially clarified by some straightforward observations. The first is the obvious fact that most persons adhere to a morality of some sort, if only in the sense that they seem sincerely to believe in the correctness of certain moral opinions. The second observation—even more obvious—is that the moralities to which people adhere differ widely, at least in their specific content. The third observation, which follows from what has already been said, is that the term *morality* is to a great extent independent in meaning from these differences in content; it may be correctly applied to sets of norms, rules, and so on, which differ sharply with each other. Thus both the Victorian moralist and the sexual libertarian have moralities, or moral codes, despite the fact that they hold contradictory views about certain sexual practices. It is this indeterminacy of content that makes it possible for an anthropologist to speak of inquiry into the morality of a culture other than his own, and for a pacifist to talk about the morality of an aggressive militarist.

It is this notion—the notion of a morality *simpliciter*—that concerns me in the following pages. The chief focus of the inquiry will be the relationship between the notion of a morality *simpliciter* and the notions of *utility, benefit, satisfaction of interest, social harmony,* and related concepts. It has been popular in recent moral philosophy to assert that there is an essential logical connection between these two sets of concepts; that nothing could count as a morality that did not to some degree espouse satisfaction of interest, social harmony, and the like. The chief purpose here is to refute such a position, and to argue for a broader conception of morality that includes codes or systems of behavior that do not have such a concern. Thus my task is largely negative, and nothing that I say, either here or later, should be construed as a claim to have achieved a definitive and complete analysis of the term *morality.* But in chapters 2 and 3 I shall undertake a fairly general survey of the application of this term, blocking out and delimiting the concept of morality to at least some degree.

Moral1 and Moral2

The sense of the question "What is a morality?" calls for more clarification before we can proceed. Let us focus for a moment not upon the noun *morality* but upon the adjective *moral.* In ordinary discourse, this latter term is used in a variety of ways. But among the various correct uses of the term, we may discern at least two "senses" or rough classes of usage. These two classes are perhaps best illustrated by two lists of specific sentences in which the term *moral* might appropriately appear:

List One

1) For Brown, whether or not one smokes tobacco is a moral issue.
2) My moral sentiments on the matter are as follows . . . .
3) Jones has a very unusual set of moral principles concerning sex.
4) You have a serious moral decision to make here.
5) He made some moral judgments with which I concur.
6) Mrs. Winterbottom seems to regard good art as simply that which reinforces her own moral prejudices.
7) You shouldn't have done that. Oh, I don't mean that what you did was wrong on moral grounds; I only mean that it wasn't very smart.
8) It is imprudent to guide foreign policy by moral considerations.
9) My moral values on questions of sexual behavior have changed radically in the past few years.
10) According to the moral principles of the Eskimos, it is acceptable under some circumstances to do away with grandparents.
11) The Chiga of Africa have moral standards that are very different from our own.
12) The moral code of the Hopi prohibits display of anger and aggressiveness within the ingroup.
13) What is for us a matter of indifference may be governed by strict moral rules in another society.

List Two
  1) He is to be praised; what he did was precisely the moral course of action.
  2) Sometimes lying may be a very moral act.
  3) Brown is, by my standards, definitely a moral person.
  4) Under no circumstances is slavery a moral practice.
  5) Some wars are moral.
  6) We often face a choice between moral behavior and selfish behavior.
  7) His intentions are quite moral.

In List One, the term *moral* is used to modify terms such as *issue, sentiment, decision, judgment, value, principle, standard, rule,* and so on. The force of the term is to classify or describe the thing characterized, without necessarily suggesting any evaluation of that thing or any value-judgment on the part of the speaker. *Moral* here is contrasted with *nonmoral.* In List Two, on the other hand, the term *moral* modifies such terms as *course of action, person, practice, intention,* and so forth. It is *normative* or *commendatory* in force; it indicates a favorable appraisal of that which it characterizes. *Moral* here is contrasted with *immoral.* The contrast between uses in the two lists is revealed by the fact that in List Two, the terms *morally right* or *morally good* may be substituted for *moral* while preserving roughly the same sense and impact of the sentences. This is not the case in List One; it would be odd, for instance, to say "For Brown, whether or not one smokes tobacco is a morally right issue."

The two uses of *moral* are exhibited together in the following sentences:

"You have a moral decision to make, between reneging on your promise, or else doing the moral thing and keeping it."

"Brown's moral code shows that he is not a moral man."

I take the liberty of distinguishing these two classes of uses of *moral* by employing subscripts in the following fashion: when *moral* is intended in the sense in which it is employed in List One, I shall speak of $moral_1$. When *moral* is intended in the sense in which it is employed in List Two, I shall speak of $moral_2$. When the context of the discussion makes the sense clear, no subscripts will be used.

Employing this convention, the two above sentences become:

"You have a $moral_1$ decision to make, between reneging on your promise, or else doing the $moral_2$ thing and keeping it."

"Brown's $moral_1$ code shows that he is not a $moral_2$ man."

Use of this convention helps to avoid the initial appearance of self-contradiction in the following sentence: "That moral principle is not a moral principle." The sentence becomes "That $moral_1$ principle is not a $moral_2$ principle."

What is it that we are saying about a person when we characterize him as *amoral*? Strictly speaking, to be amoral is not to have bad moral standards, but to have no moral standards whatsoever. Thus, to employ our convention, an amoral person is a person who has no $moral_1$ standards. It follows, incidentally, that he has no $moral_2$ standards either; for if he has no standards that constitute a moral code of any kind at all, it follows *a fortiori* that he has no standards that constitute a *good* moral code.

I shall note at a later point the tendency among some persons and groups to identify $moral_1$ with $moral_2$; that is, the tendency to refuse to count as a morality *simpliciter* anything that does not coincide with one's personal moral norms and attitudes. I defer the matter for the time being.

It is tempting simply to dub $moral_1$ as the *descriptive sense* of the term and $moral_2$ as the *normative* or *commendatory sense*. Such a way of putting the matter is probably unobjectionable so long as it is taken merely as an observation about the uses specified in List One and List Two. But it is philosophically misleading and perhaps pernicious if it is taken to suggest that a clear distinction exists between two general, clearly delineated classes of terms or statements, the descriptive and the normative. For despite the widespread appeal to a distinction of this sort in philosophical literature, no clear, decisive, and general characterization of the distinction seems available as yet. In attempting to establish a distinction between *normative discourse* and *descriptive discourse,* philosophers are prone to cite a few examples and then to fall back upon the intuitions of the reader in support of generalizations that are not adequately supported by the cited examples alone.[1] Thus, when I refer to the distinction between $moral_1$ and $moral_2$, I do not pretend to invoke some general formula by which description and evaluation might be neatly distinguished. The sense of these terms should be understood as illustrated by the specific examples cited in List One and List Two; and questions about how the terms are to be understood should be referred to those examples, rather than to some unspecified, intuitive, general distinction.

Other cautionary remarks are in order. Within List

One, use of the term *moral* may not be entirely uniform. The same remark holds for List Two. Much depends upon the context of the utterance of the sentences in these lists, and I have not specified these contexts. Full specification of context is, however, not possible here. I can only appeal to the reader to supply what he considers to be a likely or appropriate context for utterance of the sentences, and then to determine for himself whether there is a distinction to be drawn of the kind I have suggested, between a salient usage of *moral* in List One and a salient usage of *moral* in List Two.

It is perhaps worth noting, by way of further clarification, that *moral* is not the only term exhibiting an ambiguity of this kind. For instance, a person may be said to make a *prudential* decision (in the sense of a decision concerning what will serve his considered interests) that is *not* prudential (in the sense of actually being likely to serve his considered interests). Following our convention with *moral*, we might say that the person's $prudential_1$ decision was not $prudential_2$. (*$Prudential_2$* is roughly synonymous with *prudent*.) Similarly, an $aesthetic_1$ object (such as a sculpture) may be not at all $aesthetic_2$. Even the term *scientific* is ambiguous in this way. It may refer vaguely to a kind of approach to problem-solving that uses controlled empirical procedures in the attempt to explain and predict natural events, regardless of how well that approach is employed ($scientific_1$). On the other hand, to describe something as *scientific* may be to commend it as exhibiting the characteristics of good scientific procedure. Thus a $scientific_1$ study may or may not be very $scientific_2$.[2]

Restatement of the Problem

The distinction between *moral*$_1$ and *moral*$_2$ provides us with a new way of clarifying the question "What is a morality?" Let us for the moment understand *moral* as *moral*$_1$. And let us confine our attention for the moment to the morality of an individual rather than the morality of a group. Then to say that a man has a morality is to say that at least some of the following statements are true of him:

a) He is committed to some moral values, standards, principles, or rules.
b) He has some moral sentiments or attitudes.
c) He regards some issues as moral issues.
d) He is disposed under some circumstances to make moral judgments.
e) He regards certain sorts of choices as calling for a moral decision.[3]

The question "What is a morality?" may be restated as the question "How may the morality of a man be identified?" And this question may, in turn, be put in the following variety of ways, as suggested by statments 1)—5):

1) What characteristics differentiate a man's moral values, standards, principles, or rules from his other values, standards, principles or rules?
2) What characteristics differentiate a man's moral sentiments or attitudes?
3) What characteristics indicate that a man regards an issue as a moral issue rather than as an issue of another kind?

4) What characteristics differentiate a man's dispositions to make moral judgments from his dispositions to make other sor ; of judgments?

5) What characteristics indicate that a man regards certain sorts of choices as calling for a moral decision rather than a decision of another kind?

I do not wish to maintain that a satisfactory answer to any one of these questions would automatically provide a fully satisfactory answer to each of the others. Nevertheless the questions are clearly closely related to each other, and in the pages that follow it will be necessary for me to be fairly free-wheeling in moving from one formulation to another. In general, however, I concern myself chiefly with questions 2), 3), and 5), for the following reasons:

In the first place, to say that a man adheres to certain values, standards, principles, or rules may in some contexts suggest that the man is *capable of giving verbal expression* to those values, standards, and so forth in some explicit, coherent fashion. But, as I shall argue in chapter 2, a person may be properly said to have an identifiable morality even though he is unable to give an explicit, coherent expression of a moral code or set of moral values, principles, and the like. He may guide his own behavior, and judge himself and others, from the standpoint of a moral point of view that he cannot verbalize effectively. Hence I prefer the weaker, more general terms *sentiment* and *attitude,* even though they are admittedly imprecise. A person surely could not be said to have a morality unless he had some moral sentiments or attitudes. Where I do speak of a man's moral values or principles, I do not in general intend to imply that the man so described could necessarily give a full statement of an explicit moral code.

I understand the terms *sentiment* and *attitude* in a fairly broad sense, so as to include what might be called *attitudinal beliefs:* beliefs to the effect that something (or someone) has a property regarding which one has a pro- or con- attitude. And in fact, as I shall argue later, I think that $moral_1$ pro- and con- attitudes or sentiments typically have the character of property-attributing beliefs, as opposed to sheer favorable or unfavorable reactions. But these remarks call for yet another qualification: I understand *property* in a broad sense. I do not, for instance, limit properties to what ethical naturalists apparently have in mind when they declare that moral properties are definable in terms of "empirical" properties.

Note that a man may have attitudinal beliefs, that is, beliefs that attribute value-properties to things, without necessarily being able to cite any general principles constituting an explicit moral code. This is the chief reason for my preference for the terms *attitude* and *sentiment.*

As for my concentration upon questions 3) and 5): it would seem that a person's moral sentiments are best revealed by the way he regards or responds to various sorts of issues and decision-situations. To put the matter loosely, issues and choices of the proper sort "activate" a person's moral sentiments and cause him to exhibit his moral point of view. When we have ascertained what issues a person regards as moral issues and what choices a person regards as calling for a moral decision, we have essentially determined where his moral sentiments lie.

In this section I have spoken exclusively of individual morality, that is, the morality of an individual man. But the criteria I seek should be helpful in ascertaining the morality of a group or society as well. For to speak of the morality of a group is presumably to speak of a morality that is widely held or shared by members of that group.

An Analogy with the Study of Religion

I conceive of this inquiry as analogous to certain sorts of inquiries into the phenomenon of religion. At the risk of multiplying explanations to an excess, I will pursue this analogy as another way of clarifying my approach to the issue before us.

How does one approach the study of religion? Obviously there are many different standpoints from which religion might be approached. Perhaps the most common standpoints are two: a) that of the person who adheres to some particular set of religious beliefs and is engaged in stating them and promulgating them, and b) that of the person who is seeking for a set of religious beliefs that he can adopt and perhaps promulgate. By an obvious analogy, we may term such approaches *normative religion*. The attempt to state in detail the doctrines of a particular religion, to advance them to a higher theoretical level, to resolve problems implicit in them, and so on, is a great part of what is commonly called *theology*. Theology, thus understood, is an extension of normative religion.

There also occur inquiries into the meaning of religious terms (such as *faith*), and analyses of such things as the *logic of religious reasoning* and the conception of *religious knowledge*. Again using an obvious analogy, we may term these approaches *meta-religion*. They are typically done under the rubric of *philosophy of religion*, although this latter term usually covers other sorts of activity as well.

Another, rather different approach to religion is that of social anthropologists, who investigate the various religions of the world, describe them, and perhaps engage in comparisons of one religion with another. A related approach is found in courses in "comparative world religions," which may employ some anthropological data but more typically engage in interpretive and comparative studies of what might be called the basic *theologies* of various major world religions, as stated in the writings of the respective spiritual leaders of these religions. These two sorts of approach correspond to various sorts of comparative studies of moralities in different cultures.

Implicit in these last two approaches, that of the social anthropologist and that of the person doing a comparative study of world religions, is some sort of rough conception of the meaning of the word *religion*, as a descriptive term applying to a variety of usually very complex institutions that embody systems of beliefs, practices, offices, hierarchies of responsibility and status, typical sorts of attitudes, and so on. Without at least a rough conception of the meaning of the term, the field anthropologist could not select that portion of the social phenomena of a given culture which falls under the classification of *religion;* without at least a rough conception of the meaning of the term, the person engaged in research into world religions could not know what objects to include in his study.

Thus there arises the question "What is a religion?" or "What characteristics make something a religion?," and various subsidiary questions such as "What makes a belief a religious belief?," "What makes a practice a religious practice?," "What makes an attitude a religious attitude?," and so on. Although I cannot spell out answers to these questions here, social anthropologists generally operate with a reasonably satisfactory working definition of religion that has enabled them to carry out extensive, and often highly fruitful, studies of the religions of other cultures. And discussions as to how the question "What is a religion?" may be answered have not only been useful to anthropologists, but have also been of value in what I have called *normative religion* and *meta-religion* as well. A better understanding of what constitutes religion *per se* can be of definite value in the attempt to work out an acceptable set of religious beliefs and practices; and it can be especially helpful in the attempt to understand the phenomenon of religion, its modes of reasoning, the nature of its concepts, and so forth.

It may be that in order to be said to have a religion, a person must possess and employ some concept or concepts of a particular kind. One candidate might be the concept of the *divine*. If this is so, then proper use of the concept of religion in social anthropology would presuppose some understanding, at least implicit, of the concept or concepts in question. Since inquiry into key concepts of religion is part of the concern of *meta-religion*, the activities of the social anthropologist and the philosopher of religion would be importantly linked. These remarks assume special importance when we return to the analogous case of morality. Further attention will be given to the issues that arise out of them in the final section of this chapter.

Here, then, is where I place my inquiry into the notion of a morality. I wish to clarify to some degree the descriptive term *morality* as it applies to various bodies of beliefs, dispositions, sentiments, and so on. Although I shall make only a beginning, I believe that such an inquiry is at least potentially of considerable value to persons engaged in other sorts of studies of ethics. On the one hand, it may be of some value to social anthropologists, by providing a somewhat more precise conception of morality than that which they now employ. The need for greater precision in this matter is attested to by scholars who have examined anthropological discussions of morality. According to May and Abraham Edel, "Anthropology has no established definitions of the moral, nor even any body of common ascriptions."[4] And John Ladd claims that this lack of a common conception of morality has resulted in conflicting anthropological data: ". . . many of the divergencies [sic] in findings about the ethics of non-literate peoples stem from the use of totally different criteria of ethics."[5] On the other hand, a better understanding of the notion of a morality *simpliciter* may be valuable to persons engaged in normative ethics and meta-ethics; for surely attempts to specify an ideal moral code and to clarify basic ethical discourse may be enriched by a clearer idea of what constitutes a morality in the first place. Although recent English and American moral philosophy has concerned itself primarily with the attempt to analyze and understand moral discourse, its starting point has generally been discourse characteristic of a segment of the twentieth-century English-speaking public. The result, in my opinion, has frequently been comparable to the attempt to understand a portion of a machine without an adequate conception of the function and nature of the machine as a whole.

Thus an inquiry into the notion of a morality *simpliciter* has at least the potential for providing a link between two general approaches to ethics that have perhaps been too sharply divided in the past: the "scientific" or "descriptive" study of moralities, and the "philosophical" study of morality. And the result of providing this link may well be mutual illumination.

Some Difficulties Facing This Inquiry

The question of how the notion of a morality is to be understood, or how $moral_1$ is to be analyzed, should be distinguished from the factual question of whether there exists any general, cross-cultural agreement on the proper content of $moral_2$—that is, whether there are any values to which all known moralities subscribe. For if such "universal moral values" were uncovered, we would still be left with the question of whether they belonged to the very meaning of $moral_1$ or whether merely in fact all moralities countenance them. Thus, if it should be discovered that every known morality contained some prescription enjoining mothers to care for their infant children (barring unusual conditions and excusing circumstances), this fact would not in itself require us to say that *by definition* every morality enjoined such behavior; nor would it, incidentally, even entail that such behavior was actually morally right.

Nevertheless, so long as we are concerned to report actual usage rather than to advocate a "reformed" usage, it would be unwise to consider $moral_1$ and $moral_2$ as wholly unrelated in meaning. Even in those cases in ordinary language where the occurrence of *moral* may be reasonably identified as $moral_1$ (as, for instance, in "He has very strange moral views"), it must be admitted that usage differs substantially. Furthermore, a person's conception of what counts as $moral_2$ is likely to influence his conception of what counts as $moral_1$. In other words, what one believes to be morally good and bad is likely to influence what he thinks could possibly count as a morality or moral code. If the content of a code differs sufficiently from our own, we may be inclined to deny it the name *morality* altogether, despite structural and formal similarities of the two. Where there is widespread agreement among members of a cultural group as to the content of normative ethics, there is likely to occur an identification of $moral_1$ with $moral_2$. Thus medieval churchmen, sharing a fairly detailed code of morality, could regard the pagans as having no morality whatsoever. Where disputes concerning moral value abound, a more generous conception of $moral_1$ will probably be present.

It might be supposed that the issue here is simply one of tolerance versus dogmatism, open-mindedness versus ethnocentricity. But such a supposition would be a mistake. Insofar as we are reporting actual usage rather than advocating a new usage, we must follow the meaning of $moral_1$ wherever it takes us. If the result of our search is the conclusion that, say, a code of behavior of a nonliterate African tribe, although structurally and functionally similar to a morality, is *not* a morality because it is applied to the wrong sorts of things or because it lacks the appropriate concepts, this conclusion does not *ipso facto* convict us of intolerance. To deny a code the name *morality* does not entail a pejorative, unfavorable attitude toward it. We might, in fact, refuse to call a code a morality yet regard it quite favorably.[6]

Thus there is a sense in which the issue before us is "merely verbal." What does it matter, one might ask, whether or not one uses the terms *morality* or *moral* for differing codes of behavior, provided that one understands these codes, with their similarities and differences? But one of the best reasons for investigating the notion of a morality is precisely in order to elicit such an understanding; by scrutinizing the category of the moral, and by examining candidates for membership in that category, one should gain a much clearer picture of this facet of human life.

Nevertheless, the problem remains of how best to deal with the considerable fluidity of the terms *moral* and *morality*. In view of the great variation that may be found in usage of these terms, I believe it is necessary to abandon the attempt to provide a purely descriptive analysis, and to adopt, to some degree, a stipulative or reformatory approach. If we attempted to avoid any divergence whatsoever from the various generally acceptable uses of the term *morality,* our study would degenerate into a philosophically uninteresting catalogue of a great variety of only loosely related usages. Hence I propose to focus upon those characteristics of a morality which appear to me to be conceptually more central than others. My focus will not be wholly arbitrary; I will be guided partially by usage in the social sciences and partially by usage that is quite prevalent in good ordinary discourse (perhaps as a consequence of the influence of the social sciences). More will be said regarding this matter in chapter 3.

Some Further Difficulties

Early in this chapter I remarked that in this study I do not "aim to give a detailed conceptual analysis of any one, specific moral term, such as *duty, responsible,* and the like." This remark may suggest that I am attempting to do something that is logically quite distinct from what philosophers have come to call *meta-ethics*—that is, the inquiry into the meaning of key ethical terms, the logic of moral reasoning, and related matters. If such a suggestion were correct, and questions of meta-ethics were declared to be irrelevant to the topic of this study, then the prognosis for even partial success would be poor indeed. For the study would be, at its outset, open to a telling criticism. The criticism may be put as follows:[7]

The problem of how morality is to be defined cannot be divorced from traditional problems of meta-ethics. For to possess a morality is not merely to exhibit certain kinds of empirically observable behavior; it is to engage in certain sorts of conceptual activity. To possess a morality is to possess and employ concepts of a certain sort. For instance, a person could hardly be said to have a morality unless he viewed certain sorts of behavior as *right* and other sorts of behavior as *wrong*. Furthermore, he must employ these concepts of rightness and wrongness *in a particular fashion*. The fact that a man makes judgments about the right or wrong way to adjust a carburetor is not, for instance, indicative of his possession of a morality. To possess a morality, a man must employ the concepts of rightness and wrongness in that particular and specific fashion which marks them off as concepts of *moral* rightness and wrongness. Now it is just such concepts—of moral rightness and wrongness, moral duty, moral obligation, moral praiseworthiness, and so on—that have constituted a large part of the subject matter of meta-ethics. Clarification of these concepts is one of the major tasks of meta-ethics. But if to possess a morality is to employ certain sorts of concepts—*moral* concepts—and if meta-ethics concerns itself in large part with analysis of these concepts, then a definition of morality would apparently have to wait upon completion of the traditional meta-ethical tasks.

The criticism may be reinforced by consideration of attempts to avoid all meta-ethical questions in clarifying the concept of morality. Suppose it were suggested, for instance, that rule-governed behavior that entailed the possibility of self-sacrifice for the benefit of others constituted a sign of morality. Then we would have to admit that certain sorts of insects, ants, and bees, for example, exhibit signs of possessing a morality. But we are quite certain (are we not?) that ants and bees do not possess moralities, except perhaps in a metaphorical sense. And why do we feel certain that ants and bees do not possess moralities? Is it not because we are certain that they do not reason in a moral fashion, and do not employ concepts in a moral fashion? Is it not because we are certain that they do not, for instance, think of themselves and others as subject to duties and obligations, do not attribute guilt or innocence, do not praise or blame, and so on? To ascertain whether a person or group has a morality, we must ascertain whether he or it employs these concepts. And hence, to clarify the notion of a morality it would seem necessary first to clarify these concepts.

The problem is not merely one of concept clarification, but also one of clarification of moral reasoning; for how a person employs concepts in his reasoning is indicative of whether he possesses a morality. If a person declares that one action is right and another wrong, but admits that the actions are in all other respects indistinguishable, it should be apparent that what he is saying is not the expression of a moral point of view.

How are we to meet this general line of criticism? If correct, it would seem to require us to abandon the attempt to clarify the concept of morality in general, and return to some aspect of the traditional tasks of meta-ethics; for these latter would seem to be logically prior to the inquiry into the notion of morality; and the tasks of meta-ethics are far from being fully completed.

By way of reply, I must begin by agreeing to a considerable extent with the thrust of the criticism. I believe we should not be willing to declare that someone had a morality unless we were reasonably confident that he employed roughly the same set of basic concepts that we employ in our own moral reasoning. If a man does not, for instance, make judgments about what sorts of actions are right or wrong, and what sorts of dispositional characteristics are praiseworthy or blameworthy, then I think we should not say that he has a morality.

It is worth remarking that this matter is distinct from the question of whether the man shares our particular moral standards. The question is not whether he agrees with us regarding *which* actions are right or wrong and *which* dispositions are praiseworthy or blameworthy. He may apply these terms to quite a different set of things, thereby disagreeing with us in his moral standards, and yet still possess a morality, *providing that he means at least roughly the same thing we do by the terms.*

An analogy with aesthetics may be useful here. To oversimplify the matter considerably (and perhaps even to falsify it), let us say that a man has an *aesthetic code of value*—that is, a code of value that he employs in order to evaluate various things from an aesthetic point of view—only if he employs concepts of the *beautiful,* the *sublime,* the *fitting,* and their respective opposites. Now a man may apply these concepts in a quite different way from the way we do; he may, for instance, regard something as ugly that we regard as beautiful, and vice versa.

Yet we credit him with an aesthetic code of value nevertheless, provided that he does at least employ the concepts of *beauty,* and so on. On the other hand, if he entirely lacks the concepts of the beautiful, sublime, and fitting, then he would not be said to have an aesthetic code at all.

(A qualification is in order here of the kind made in the previous section. It must be admitted that if another person's aesthetic taste differs sufficiently from our own, we may credit him with no aesthetic taste whatsoever. Where is the line to be drawn between those whom we regard as having *bad* aesthetic taste, and those whom we regard as having *no* aesthetic taste? This admission does not, however, undermine the point being presently discussed, but rather supports it. For suppose that a person predicates the terms *beautiful, sublime,* and *fitting* of so radically a different class of objects from the class of objects of which we predicate the terms that we are inclined to deny that he has an aesthetic code at all. I suggest that the reason we are inclined to deny that he has an aesthetic code is that the enormous disparity in his use of aesthetic terms *makes us doubt that he has the same concepts as we do.* And it is because we suspect that he lacks our concepts that we deny that he has an aesthetic code. His application of the terms *beautiful, sublime,* and *fitting* makes us doubt that he knows what the words mean.)

Thus the enterprise of clarifying the concept of a morality cannot be separated from the traditional tasks of meta-ethics. To move in the direction of clarifying the concept of morality is to move in the direction of clarifying basic moral concepts. What remains to be argued, therefore, is that the task that this study sets for itself is a manageable one, and may reasonably and fruitfully be undertaken here.

My first observation is that the criticism made at the beginning of this section was misleading, in that it spoke of *two* tasks, one "logically prior" to the other. It was claimed that resolution of the traditional meta-ethical problems must *precede* clarifications of the concept of morality. But the upshot of the ensuing discussion has been that to clarify the basic concepts of morality is to clarify the concept of morality itself, and vice versa. We have not two separate tasks, then, but one general task, which may be approached in a variety of ways, and which may perhaps be divided into parts.

A second observation is this: there appears to be no single term that is *exclusively* moral in import. The most central moral terms in English are perhaps *right, wrong, duty, obligation, praiseworthy,* and *blameworthy.* Now, it is obvious that *right* and *wrong* are widely used in non-moral contexts. As for *duty,* what of such uses as in "The duties of a quartermaster are as follows . . ." or "One of the duties of the pitcher is to cover home plate on passed balls"? These are not, I suggest, *necessarily* duties of moral import, though they may be regarded as morally significant by some persons. Turning to *obligation:* one may have a "social obligation" to invite the neighbors in for dinner, or to write a thank-you note, without being under the onus of a *moral* obligation. And one may be under a *legal* obligation that is not morally binding. Not all obligations are moral obligations. As for praise and blame, they are freely applied in many nonmoral contexts. For instance, the infielder who drops a pop fly will be blamed by his fans, but not necessarily in a moral sense.

Furthermore, even if there were a term that had proper application only in moral contexts, there is no assurance that the concept represented by such a term would be *logically central* to morality, and such that all other moral concepts would be definable in terms of it.

Actually existing moral codes differ with respect to which concepts they place in the forefront of moral reasoning. To cite only one kind of variation: for some persons, the concept of moral *duty* is foremost; for others, the concept of *good* has more prominence, and duties are understood as rules for the production of good.

What we seem to have, therefore, is a loosely knit family of terms, each one of which has nonmoral as well as moral uses. We are interested in characterizing their moral uses; in other words, we are interested in those uses in which they express moral concepts. Our problem is not to provide a full analysis of any one of the concepts in question, but to inquire into the distinguishing characteristics that mark them off as moral concepts, and that locate them within the family of moral discourse. We are not seeking a full analysis of the concepts of right, duty, obligation, and the like; we are, instead, seeking the criteria that delimit these concepts to moral contexts. We are interested in the species of morality, which is a part of a larger genus of normative discourse; and what is required is not that the genus as a whole be defined, but that the differentiae of the species be identified or at least illuminated to some degree.

By way of further defense of my approach, I return to the analogy with aesthetics. In order to differentiate aesthetic evaluation from other varieties of evaluation, is it necessary that full definitions first be achieved of the concepts of the beautiful, sublime, and fitting? I think not. In fact, aesthetic theory has perhaps been somewhat hindered and misled by undue preoccupation with the concept of beauty. Rather than singling out one or two of a cluster of aesthetic concepts and focusing all of one's attention on those concepts alone, might it not be more fruitful to step back and inquire into the cluster as a whole, to ask what unifies the concepts that form that cluster, and to seek a kind of general understanding of aesthetic discourse *qua* aesthetic discourse? To be sure, such a general understanding would not constitute a detailed analysis of any one of the members of the cluster. But it might very well serve as a helpful conceptual backdrop against which to pursue more detailed analyses. It is precisely because of the connection of the concept of aesthetics with specific aesthetic concepts such as that of beauty, that a general understanding of aesthetic evaluation should advance one's understanding of the concept of beauty and other specific aesthetic concepts.

To cite another, cruder analogy: if our object is to know a country better, we may begin with a single spot (perhaps the capital of the country) and examine it minutely, expanding our efforts slowly from that focal center. But it may also serve some purpose to do an aerial inspection of the country as a whole, surveying its boundaries, and learning in general what geographical configurations mark it off and distinguish it from other countries. If our lives are spent within the country and our gaze is forever fixed on a portion of it, we may in one sense know the country quite well, but in another sense know it only poorly.

Thus, as I see my enterprise here, I have something useful to contribute by the attempt to clarify the general category of moral evaluation. If successful, this attempt will move in the direction of a better understanding of specific moral concepts. It is thus importantly involved in the traditional meta-ethical tasks. On the other hand, it makes no pretense of doing a full analysis of any of these concepts. Nor, if I am correct, is a full analysis of specific moral concepts necessary in order that the category of morality be helpfully illuminated to some degree.

To be sure, if there are certain concepts that are logically central to the notion of a morality, then these concepts should gradually emerge from our study. And, in fact, the importance of certain typically moral concepts will become apparent as the discussion proceeds. By the end of chapter 3, I will have narrowed my focus somewhat, to the concepts of right and wrong behavior, and good and bad dispositional traits. But, as I will explicitly acknowledge, to talk of right and wrong behavior and good and bad traits is not yet to talk *specifically* moral talk. These concepts are not exclusively moral, but extend over a broad nonmoral range as well. It will be the task of yet later chapters to examine in a critical fashion some further claims concerning the differentiae that supposedly mark off the moral from the nonmoral.

Thus, I think it premature to insist that at this early point in the discussion, key moral concepts be singled out as definitive of a morality. It is one of the goals of this study to focus in a progressively more specific fashion upon concepts that appear to be characteristically moral. If successful, the study should *in the end* help us to clarify what it is about moral discourse that makes it characteristically moral discourse. The subject matter is meta-ethical in character; but the approach is a movement from the macroscopic to the microscopic, and not vice versa. And the movement will take us only a little way toward greater understanding of morality. It will decidedly *not* lead us to a detailed, fully complete analysis of any single ethical concept. Such an analysis is beyond the scope of this study. Yet I believe, for the reasons given, that the study may be useful nevertheless.

This brings me finally back to a point made earlier. I repeat that what I have to say is quite provisional and preliminary in nature. All I can hope to have done is to have blocked out the notion of morality to a rough degree. And my concern is with the relationship of the notion of morality to a rather specific set of concepts, those having to do with benefit, welfare, social harmony, and the like. Although I believe that this relationship is especially illuminating, I do not maintain that the exploration of it here carries us all the way to a definition of morality. As mentioned earlier, the final chapters will be largely negative in import; they will seek to refute a popular supposition about what marks help to define the moral.

As for chapter 2, its primary purpose is to provide a brief survey of some of the many important ways in which moralities may differ. It is hoped that such a survey will have several useful results:

a) A review of how moralities may differ from one another may help to forestall an overly narrow, parochial analysis of the concept of morality, by supplying a sense of the richness and diversity of morality that any analysis of the term should accommodate.

b) At the same time the citation of various phenomena to which the term *morality* may be applied will help to give some idea of how I propose to delimit the concept of morality. In List One above, a number of instances were given of a particular usage of the term *moral*. Chapter 2 should help to enrich and expand upon that list, by providing more fully described contexts for possible application of the terms *moral* and *morality*. Chapter 2 is, thus, "finitistic" in spirit;[8] that is, it seeks to avoid overly general discussions that appeal to a vaguely conceived "realm of moral discourse" in favor of concentration upon contexts in which the terms $moral_1$ and *morality* might reasonably be employed. These contexts are, admittedly, often stated in quite general terms.

c) In addition to specification of some dimensions of variation in morality, chapter 2 offers some preliminary remarks on the significance of these variations for attempts to define the concept of morality.

1. In making these observations I am influenced by an article by Professor Morton White, "A Finitistic Approach to Philosophical Theses," in *Philosophical Review* 60 (1951): 299-316. Professor White's suggestions have also influenced the way in which I set up the general problem for this inquiry. I am, of course, responsible for any respects in which I may have misconstrued what he has to say in this article.

2. This observation was prompted by remarks on the term *scientific* made by John Ladd, in *The Structure of a Moral Code* (Cambridge, Mass.: Harvard University Press, 1957), pp. 74f.

3. It may be felt that a person might have mere moral opinions about matters without having any inclination to act upon them, and that such a person could hardly be said to have a morality. On the other hand, some philosophers have maintained that assent to a moral principle *entails* having a disposition to act upon it. There has been considerable attention to this question in the literature, stimulated chiefly by R. M. Hare's *The Language of Morals* (New York: Galaxy, Oxford University Press, 1964; first published by Oxford: Clarendon Press, 1952). See especially pp. 19f. and 169; see also P. L. Gardiner, "On Assenting to a Moral Principle," *Proceedings of the Aristotelian Society* 55 (1954-1955): 23-44. I hope to skirt most of the issues that arise here (such as criteria of sincerity, and analyses of the notion of "strength of will"). In general, I will take it for granted that to have a morality entails both a) having some moral sentiments or attitudes, and b) having some dispositions to judge and act out of those sentiments and attitudes, given appropriate circumstances.

4. May Edel and Abraham Edel, *Anthropology and Ethics: The Quest for Moral Understanding*, rev. ed. (Cleveland, Ohio: The Press of Case Western Reserve University, 1968), p. 7. In this book, the Edels make a convincing case for the need for greater cross-disciplinary awareness in the study of morality.

5. Ladd, *The Structure of a Moral Code,* p. 61.

6. An example of such an attitude may be found in the ethical writings of Friedrich Nietzsche, where there occurs a vacillation between a narrow and a broad sense of $moral_1$. In advocating a new and higher kind of life, Nietzsche

sometimes speaks of himself as advocating a new morality, sometimes as proposing an alternative to morality altogether.

7. For the raising of this criticism, and for much of the way in which the criticism is put, I am indebted to Professor Roderick Firth.

8. See White, "A Finitistic Approach to Philosophical Theses."

2
The Diversity of Moralities

Introductory Remarks

As indicated at the close of chapter 1, the main purpose of this chapter is to spell out briefly, and in a somewhat schematic fashion, some of the possible variations in morality—variations that may be internal to a single morality, so that it is not entirely homogeneous; and external variations, variations from one morality to another. Description of these dimensions of variation may serve both to enrich our understanding of morality and to delimit our approach to it somewhat. In this chapter I also begin the constructive work of the inquiry by discussing, in a preliminary way, the implications of variation in moralities for different sorts of attempts to define the concept of morality. Not only is my treatment brief and schematic; it is also incomplete in another way. For I do not attempt to review all of the significant ways in which moralities may vary, but only those variations which seem to me to be of chief importance in any attempt to clarify the concept of morality itself.[1] The need for such a review arises from the fact that attempts to define morality often lose sight of the considerable variety of moral phenomena, and as a consequence fix upon an overly restrictive set of characteristics. It should be easier to avoid this kind of error if we have before us at least a brief survey of some of the dimensions of variation in morality.

This procedure would seem, however, to be open to a serious objection, which may be stated as follows: "You propose to present a variety of *instances* of morality, in order to facilitate a *definition* of morality. But pending a definition of the concept, you have no logical grounds for citing your examples as genuine instances that should fall under the definition. In fact, the whole approach is question-begging. For if you are to generalize about morality on the basis of selected instances of morality, you must already have a tacit conception of morality that has guided your selection of instances."

The objection is not so damaging as it may initially appear. In the first place, we may largely circumvent it by regarding the cited instances only as *candidates for membership* in the category of morality; whether or not they are definitely included will depend upon the final analysis of the notion of morality. Second, the concept of morality is not an entirely mysterious one; it is, rather, a concept that we already partially understand in an incomplete and intuitive way. The object of this inquiry is not to propose a radically new conception of morality, but instead to clarify and make more precise a tacit conception that we already have. Although some revision of the concept of morality may be called for, any final definition should accommodate at least the paradigm cases of morality as recognized by our preanalytic conception of it. Consequently, it is entirely appropriate to begin an analysis of the notion of morality with putative examples of moral phenomena.

Dimensions of Variation

The following, then, are some (*only* some) of the dimensions in which moralities may vary, accompanied by some observations concerning the significance of these variations for attempts to define morality.

Specific Content

Moralities differ from one another most obviously in the specific sorts of things they favor and disfavor. What for one man is a moral matter is for another man morally indifferent; what for one man is morally abhorrent may even for another man be morally obligatory. Whether, at the most general level, the content of all or most moralities coincides to some degree (as, for instance, in some sort of prohibition concerning homicide) is a difficult question that I will not resolve.[2] But when it comes to the specific expression of a morality in its day-to-day rules and standards, the variation is so apparent that we need not rehearse it here; one cannot become an adult in today's pluralistic world without the fact of moral differences becoming obvious, often even painfully so.

It is worth noting in passing that this fact would seem to bode ill for any attempt to define morality in terms of the specific sorts of actions, practices, institutions, and so on that it evaluates and regulates. For instance, does morality by definition regulate sexual behavior in some way? But there are codes that it seems reasonable to call moral codes, but that concern themselves in no special way with sexual matters. For some persons with perfectly identifiable moralities, sexual behavior *per se* is simply not a moral matter.

Character of More General Principles Appealed to

It is frequently supposed that moralities may be identified by the character of the general principles used to justify particular value judgments. In recent philosophical literature, the most popular candidates for the definitively moral principles appealed to have been rationales that appeal to something like the notion of social utility or general welfare, or perhaps general social harmony.[3] Such an account is initially attractive, especially if one is an "enlightened," Western-educated moralist whose own personal moral views are grounded in some ideal of social welfare. But a quick survey of what are at least strong candidates for the status of a morality should raise some serious doubts about this criterion. For putative moralities differ greatly in the principles or rationale offered in their support by those who adhere to them. Simple obedience to the will of one's god or gods, reverence for one's ancestors, respect for the eternal voice of Reason or Nature—these are but a few of the more popular kinds of principles that are offered in support of what would seem to be properly called moral codes. But the final chapters of this study will examine in detail the question of whether moralities are to be defined in terms of their appeal to a particular kind of higher normative principle, and discussion of the various possible answers to such a question will best be deferred until these later chapters.

There is, however, one remark that should be made here concerning what may be called "justification" of value judgments. "Justification" of a favorable or unfavorable reaction may mean one of at least two different varieties of appeal. The first, which I have mentioned above, is appeal to some higher normative principles (e.g., "This is wrong because it causes unhappiness, and whatever causes unhappiness is wrong"). The second, which I have not mentioned, makes no such appeal to normative principles but instead attempts to establish something about the logical character of the judgment (e.g., that it is "universalizable"). Now, I cannot at this point enter into the involved discussions of generalization in ethical discourse; but I find it necessary to suggest here that *some* sort of principle of generalization seems necessary in discourse that is to count as moral discourse. The principle may be no more than a *ceteris paribus* principle to the effect that in relevantly similar circumstances a similar reaction would be called for. Without such a principle in operation, I think we should begin to doubt whether a person was truly employing moral concepts.

Rationality versus Feeling

It seems often possible to ascertain a person's moral sentiments even though he himself cannot offer any significant defense of them. A morality is often adhered to largely as a matter of feeling, without issuing to any significant degree on a rational level. The extent to which a morality is or is not expressed on a rational level—that is, as a set of consciously entertained rules and standards of a self-aware person, systematized and integrated with each other, and backed up by some sort of rationale—is a matter of some importance for any attempt to define morality. Failure to recognize that moralities vary in their degree of rationality while still remaining moralities has probably increased the confusion present in philosophical debates about theories of morality. For instance, if "intuitionism" is understood as the doctrine that moral principles are somehow directly felt or "seen" to be correct, without one's being able to give any higher normative principles in support of them, then institutionism is surely true, taken as a description of a large portion of the morally sensitive public. In this group, there are persons who "intuit" the moral properties of individual matters but who have no sense of the moral correctness of general ethical principles; and there are persons whose moral intuitions operate at this latter, more general level. The point at which a person rests upon his moral intuitions, his moral sense or "feel" for moral matters, is largely a function of the degree of rationality of his morality. And a highly rational, philosophical, and nonintuitive morality is also possible. In one such type of morality, the raw, intuitive feel of moral correctness or incorrectness largely drops away in favor of a dispassionate appraisal of persons, actions, institutions, and so on, in the light of how they conform to some abstractly conceived moral ideals that one chooses to affirm. Thus intuitionism, at least as described above, would seem to be a correct description of only a part of actually existing moralities. And to insist that it correctly characterizes *any* morality is to overlook the degree to which moralities may vary in their level of rationality.

There is, of course, an important distinction between the question of how people actually do arrive at their specific moral judgments, and the question of how a moral judgment is properly or ideally arrived at. One might recognize that only a portion of the morally sensitive public intuit their basic moral principles in the sense described above, yet hold that intuitionism should be the basis for *all* moral judgment; or, alternatively, that such an intuitive foundation for morality is *never* appropriate or ideal. These issues—how people do ground their moral views, and how they should ground their moral views—are logically distinct. Most traditional intuitionist theories have been proposed less as descriptions of how people actually do ground their moral judgments than as theories about how moral judgments *must* or *should* be grounded. Nevertheless, a fair understanding of the variety of ways, rational and nonrational, in which moral judgments are actually arrived at may help to forestall an overly narrow, limited answer to the question of their proper or correct derivation.

Similar remarks to those on intuitionism above would seem to hold for emotive theories of ethics. For many persons, morality seems to consist of a rather elementary set of emotional reactions, favorable or unfavorable, to various matters.[4] Between two such persons, an ethical dispute is hardly rational, since neither moral sentiment is expressed or defended in a rational way. Again, however, this theory seems incorrect if taken as the claim that moralities everywhere fit this elementary emotive pattern. Among reflective, rational persons, morality may go far beyond a set of simply emotional reactions; it may be a highly articulated system that is consciously and rationally integrated into a total way of life and adhered to for rather intellectual reasons. Again, the observation that emotivism is a correct description of the morality of at least a segment of the morally sensitive public does not logically entail any conclusions about the only *proper* or *correct* foundation for moral judgments.

Morality as Visceral Reaction

The notion of an almost totally nonrational morality deserves some careful attention in any attempt to characterize the concept of morality. Stripped of its rational superstructure, morality may appear as little more than a set of dispositions to react in a visceral way to various sorts of things.[5] Even if a person is able to give a quite reflective, rational account of his moral opinions when required to do so, his day-to-day moral responses are nevertheless likely to be more visceral and emotive than rational in character. And most of us, from time to time, experience moral reactions for which we cannot readily provide any particularly rational account or defense. How would the reader react to hearing harsh, angry obscenities? To observing sexual exhibitionism? To encountering especially disturbing violations of good manners? If not these cases, then others will probably call forth a moral reaction, mild or severe, that is rather nonrational in character. An understanding of nonrational or visceral morality is especially important for any clarification of the concept of morality, since here one may confront morality in its most elementary, unelaborated form.

When one attends to this kind of expression of morality, it is tempting to see morality in one of two ways that are quite at odds with each other. I shall term them respectively *morality as natural good health* and *morality as compulsive neurosis*. It will be worthwhile to examine at some length these two conflicting accounts of what nonrational morality is.

Morality as natural good health. Both Plato and Aristotle understood morality in such a way that it was practically synonymous with good mental health. To be a good or virtuous man was to have a properly ordered, properly functioning *psyche*. Modern philosophers are far less likely to assume that a psychologically healthy man will be *ipso facto* a morally good man. But echoes of something like the ancient claim are still to be found, not only in modern moral philosophy but in modern clinical psychology as well. The apparent connection between morality and good mental health is best illustrated by that variety of mental illness known as the psychopathic personality. The psychopathic personality, a clinically recognized category of psychosis, is generally defined or characterized in morally significant terms. A psychopath typically has no capacity for empathy, no ability to play the role of other persons in such a way as to be affected in his behavior by a sense of sympathy for them. He is "... chronically antisocial ... always in trouble ... and maintaining no real loyalties to any person, group, or code ... frequently callous and hedonistic, showing marked emotional immaturity, with lack of sense of responsibility ..."[6] "The psychopath expresses normal reactions (love, loyalty, gratitude, etc.) with a most impressive appearance of sincerity and depth, but the emotional ties and the attitudes he professes fail to deter him from deeds that continually contradict his verbal claims. There appears to be in him a strange lack of insight or, perhaps more accurately, a total lack of one of the dimensions that constitute insight."[7] He displays "lack of remorse or shame ... inability to love another, and pathological egocentricity ... shallowness and poverty in the major human emotions."[8] The category of the psychopathic personality was, in fact, for many years referred to simply as *moral insanity.*"[9]

It is obvious that the personality characteristics that are lacking in the psychopathic personality are characteristics that are central to morality as we usually understand it. How can an individual be said to have a morality if he has no conscience, no sense of responsibility, no capacity for sympathy or love, and is thoroughly egocentric? Certainly we tend to believe that to have a morality is, after all, to exhibit a certain dimension or range of human emotional responses, and that a person who fails to exhibit this dimension of responses is not simply reprehensible but actually defective in a fundamental way. It may seem reasonable, in fact, to regard these psychological characteristics as the defining characteristics of a morality wherever it appears, and to reaffirm the ancient equation of morality and mental health.

But such a conclusion would be premature. Whatever their basis in the "natural" psychology of the species, moralities are also complex social inventions, displaying all of the richness, articulation, inconsistency, and susceptibility to curious convolutions that are characteristic of any biological interest when it develops into the social realm. Sometimes the end result of this development is so bizarre or perverse that it is hardly recognizable as an extrapolation from the original elementary human interest.

Furthermore, we may ask whether the mere presence of dispositions to empathize, to sympathize, to feel loyalty to others, to love, and the like, is sufficient in itself to constitute having a morality. As a way of answering this question, consider the hypothetical case of a man we will call Taylor. Taylor is, we would say, a man without any principles. He feels no sense of honor or responsibility when it comes to dealing with people in general; he behaves simply as he pleases, and as it benefits him. He has no internalized sense of right and wrong and never feels guilt, insofar as guilt is understood as a sense of pain at having behaved in a way that is justifiably liable to criticism. But Taylor has a small circle of friends whom he sincerely loves. He is generous with them, he sympathizes with them in their difficulties, and he is quite loyal to them. His generosity, sympathy, and loyalty arise, however, not out of any sense of moral rightness or goodness, but simply out of his immediate inclinations. He behaves as he does simply because he likes to.

It is natural to say that Taylor is "not all bad," and as evidence point to his relationship with his friends. It is even natural to say that he is to some extent a moral person. But it is not natural, I suggest, to say that he *has a morality.* The case of Taylor illuminates a distinction that I will mark off as the distinction between *feeling or acting in a morally approved way,* and *having a morality.*[10] The distinction is a basic one, and is important to note here. For we are concerned not with the conditions under which it is correct to say that a person has behaved in a morally approved way, but with the conditions under which it is correct to say that a person has a morality. What was lacking in Taylor was any sense of *acting from an internalized set of values, of doing the right thing because it was right,* and not simply because he felt like doing it. Taylor is not a psychopath, for he possesses those dimensions of personality which the psychopath lacks; but Taylor does not have a morality.

These observations cast additional light on the notion of morality as natural good health. To have a morality is not simply to have certain benevolent dispositions; it is, rather, to have a disposition to judge and act out of a sense of the rightness or goodness of certain sorts of behavior.[11] A person may be a highly moral person (in the sense that everything he enjoys doing and is inclined to do happens to be in accordance with good moral principles), yet have no morality (in that he is never motivated to act out of a sense of the right or good).

When one clearly understands the centrality to the concept of morality of this latter feature, the motivation to act out of a sense of the right and the good, then one realizes that elementary morality cannot be defined simply in terms of a natural disposition to feel empathy, benevolence, and other such emotions. Indeed, it is possible for a person to be inculcated into a morality that repudiates these gentle emotions in favor of some austere and aggressive ideals. For such a person, there may be no virtue in sympathy or generosity. Virtue may lie, rather, in strict adherence to the stern code of honor that he has been taught and that he believes to be binding upon all men.

We must remind ourselves of a point that has become obscured in the above discussion: our concern is not with $moral_2$ but with $moral_1$. It may be reasonable to hold that all *acceptable* or *admirable* moralities build upon and affirm the gentle, benevolent emotions. But it is not the case, I believe, that *all* moralities do so. In order for a person to have a morality, it is surely necessary that he have at least some slight disposition or motivation to judge and act out of what he feels to be good and right, where *good* and *right* are not simply other names for what he feels personally inclined to do or finds prudent to do. A sense of the good and the right need not coincide with any empathetic or sympathetic emotions. Whatever causal connection there may be between possession of the benevolent, empathetic emotions and development of a morality, I would suggest that there is no essential logical connection between them.

By way of reinforcement of this claim, let us consider a possible moral code that would seem to place no value upon sympathy or benevolence. Suppose a group of men who adhere to a strict code of behavior governing every major aspect of their lives together. Suppose that adherence to this code is considered a matter of honor, and violations of the code are met with general group sanctions, including severe ostracism. Suppose that persons in the group who violate the code are prone to exhibit distinct signs f remorse and guilt. Suppose that the code frequently and typically calls for sacrifice of self-interest. Suppose, finally, that the code is held to be binding upon all men solely because it is held to derive from the will of a supreme being who has created all men, and who has no other interest save that his will be obeyed. Considerations of the welfare of members of the group are irrelevant to the rightness of the code. In fact, if adherence to the code were incidentally to result in the painful death of every member of the group (perhaps in the course of defending a religious shrine), this fact would be regarded as irrelevant to the correctness of the code. Furthermore, whether or not one person displays benevolence toward another is of no particular concern to the supreme being, and hence of no particular importance in the code. Benevolent behavior may be practiced by members of the group, but simply as a matter of taste or preference, not as a matter of moral right and wrong.

Although the description of this hypothetical code is not very complete, I believe that the reader may fill out the account readily enough and may come to agree that such a code a) could exist; b) could properly be called a *moral*$_1$ code; and c) would not place any particular moral value upon benevolence or sympathy, except perhaps as techniques for inculcation of the code. It may well be the case that a person growing up within a group adhering to such a code might never adopt the code for himself and internalize it as a part of his own set of values unless he had some capacity for empathy or role-playing, and some need for benevolence (so that his behavior might be influenced by displays of good will or its absence to him on the part of other members of the group). But this is only to say that empathy and benevolence would then be *causal preconditions* for the internalization of the code, not that empathy and benevolence were in part *definitive* of the code.

Such a code is undoubtedly not very attractive to us. But I reiterate that this, if it is the case, is beside the point. The question is not "What is an acceptable moral code?" but "What is a conceivable moral code?" And, acceptable or not, the code I have described is not very different from certain codes, based largely upon the Old Testament, that have occurred in the Judao-Christian tradition.

Morality as compulsive neurosis. The preceding discussion began with an attempt to understand nonrational morality as "visceral reaction." The first suggestion, which has now been rejected, is that to have a nonrational morality is simply to possess certain benevolent dispositions—inclinations to empathize, to sympathize, and so on. This account, while it helped to clarify the minimal conditions for "being a moral person" or "feeling and acting in a morally approved way" (as viewed from the vantage point of a particular, fairly attractive set of moral values), proved not to satisfy the conditions for actually having a morality. What was lacking was the sense of rightness of goodness as a source of motivation for one's judgments and/or actions. If we now turn to *this* feature of having a morality and attempt to analyze it as it appears on a primitive level, it begins to look quite different from the natural, healthy benevolent dispositions. It bears certain striking similarities, in fact, to *neurotic* syndromes such as compulsive behavior. The similarity becomes apparent when we attend carefully to the phenomenological character of nonrational moral sentiments and visceral moral reactions. Consider an actual case of a nonrational negative moral reaction to, say, some radical breach of good manners. One feels troubled or disturbed; the breach creates an uneasiness and dissatisfaction; things have been put out of kilter. The proper order of things has been violated, and must somehow be responded to and righted. The internalized standard to which one adheres, and which has been violated, seems to control the *gestalt* of one's perception of the event. The breach has not simply been *judged* to be wrong; the very percept of the breach emanates a kind of wrongness. This sense of wrongness has definite phenomenological similarities to the dissatisfaction and anxiety that a neurotically compulsive person supposedly feels when things are not as his neurosis commands they should be. The table should not be disorderly; it must be reordered. The hands should not be dirty; they must be washed. The sidewalk cracks should not be stepped upon; they must be avoided. Are not these experiences similar in character to the visceral moral reaction against sexual exhibitionism, or petty dishonesty, or many other moral transgressions? One has internalized a standard and has in a sense *become addicted to it.* It governs not simply the way one judges about things, but the way one feels or perceives on a prerational level.

The persistent foothold that a moral standard may gain in one's visceral reactions to things may often, in fact, resist any rational attempts to oppose it. It is not uncommon to hear a person say something like "I know I have no good reason to feel guilty, but I can't help myself."

It is this feature of morality that yields most of whatever plausibility is contained in a libertarian's claim that "All morality is just a psychological hang-up." It would also seem to be this feature of morality (among others) that Nietzsche had in mind in much of his railing against conventional morality—which he often seems to regard in just the sort of way we typically regard neurotic behavior. And a reputable contemporary moral philosopher, in discussing how morality is experienced, has even been led to remark that ". . . morality may be no more than the manifestation of a socially useful compulsive neurosis. . . ."[12]

But whatever the similarities between visceral moral reactions and compulsive behavior, there are also important—in fact, probably decisive—dissimilarities, at least in their paradigm manifestations. The clinically recognized category of compulsive neurosis is that of "obsessive-compulsive disorder" and a psychologist defines it as "one of the reaction types of psychoneurosis in which the individual suffers from the need to perform either logically unnecessary ritualistic acts (compulsions) or experiences repugnant thought (obsessions)."[13] Furthermore, a compulsive person experiences a need or drive to repeat his compulsive behavior, even if he recognizes its irrationality.[14] Thus paradigm cases of compulsive neuroses differ from paradigm cases of nonrational moral reactions in the following ways:

1) The compulsive person feels *compelled to act* in certain senseless ways; indeed, it is this compulsion to *perform strange actions* that goes to define his disorder. A moral reaction, on the other hand, need be no more than an emotional event that gives rise to no action at all. And where a moral reaction does give rise to action, the action is often reluctant, and taken in opposition to inclinations, rather than as a result of compelling psychological drives. (Not "I just have to . . ." but rather "I don't want to, but I suppose I should. . . .")

2) Compulsive behavior is defined as *irrational:* as senseless, unnecessary, and inappropriate. But while moral reactions may often be irrational and inappropriate, they need not be; much of morally reactive behavior appears to fulfill quite an appropriate and necessary function in social interaction. Moral reactions do not seem to be senseless and out of place in the way that compulsive behavior is.

3) The differences described in both 1) and 2) above are captured in the observation that compulsive behavior is *repetitious and ritualistic,* whereas normal moral reaction is not. In moral reaction there is typically no analogue of neurotic behavior such as an incessant need to wash one's hands.

4) Compulsive behavior is typically motivated by distress, anxiety, and the desire to rectify or compensate for some undesirable state; it is, in short, typically motivated by a *negative* reaction of some sort. Moral reaction, on the other hand, is not always negative; it may be positive or favorable as well. Something like the spontaneous moral outburst of appreciation and approval of an act of generosity would seem to have no analogue in compulsive behavior. Even where moral reaction is negative, it is more characteristically motivated by something like indignation than by anxiety.

5) Finally, a disposition to react in a moral fashion may be an adjunct to a life that is healthy and functional by every usual standard; and the capacity for moral sensitivity may actually contribute to the health and success of the individual. Compulsive behavior, on the other hand, is typically dysfunctional and disruptive; it is counterproductive of the agent's personal satisfactions and his successful interaction with others.

In the face of these differences, the similarities be-

tween moral reaction and compulsive behavior dwindle
to the bare fact that, in both, one possesses a sense of
how things should be and therefore reacts negatively to
situations that are not congruent with this sense. To be
sure, moral reactions may become neurotic and compulsive. But they need not be; to characterize them as
essentially compulsive would be, I think, a serious error.

Review. The discussion of morality as "visceral reaction" has been a long and somewhat rambling one. But
there are, I believe, good reasons for an extended attention to this kind of expression of morality. For 1) in the
lives of many persons, morality operates almost wholly
on this nonrational level, as a rather specialized set of
emotive, intuitive responses and dispositions. Even
among persons who are capable, when pressed, of giving
some sort of rational account of their moral sentiments,
their day-to-day moral reactions are not likely to be
thoroughly imbued with this rational awareness. Any account of what morality is must take cognizance of this
fact, and display some understanding of what morality is
on the nonrational level. Furthermore, 2) not all
moralities are rational but presumably all moralities
must contain basic moral sentiments and give rise to
basic moral reactions of some sort.[15] It would seem,
therefore, that what is common to and definitive of all
morality must be found within this elementary level of
moral expression. Consequently it is important for our
purposes that it be scrutinized carefully. Finally, 3) the
notion of a nonrational morality is all too easily confused
with some other notion, such as that of psychological
good health on the one hand or psychological hang-ups
and compulsions on the other. It is important, therefore,
to distinguish as clearly as possible between these notions
and what it is to have a nonrational morality.

The results of this section may be summarized as follows: Observation of how moralities may vary in the degree to which they issue on a rational level led to an inquiry into the notion of nonrational or visceral morality. Two accounts of visceral morality were examined and rejected. The first, morality as natural good health, was unsatisfactory because it failed to encompass an essential characteristic of any morality, that of some degree of motivation to judge and act out of a sense of the right and the good. And a sense of the right and the good may, in some moralities, be at odds with the supposedly healthy empathetic and sympathetic dispositions. Thus, the notion of morality as natural good health is not neutral regarding morality *simpliciter;* it derives rather from a particular sort of conception of moral value. It reflects an intrusion of a conception of moral$_2$ into the analysis of moral$_1$.

Attention to visceral morality as motivation to act out of an elementary sense of the right and good led to a comparison of moral reactions with compulsive neurosis. Although there appear to be compelling analogies between these two phenomena, and some moral theorists have apparently suggested that they may be identical, various dissimilarities between them were held in the end to overrule any reduction of moral reaction to compulsive neurosis.

Levels of Moral Development
in the Individual

The infant child can hardly be said to have a morality; yet, by the time he becomes an adult, he is likely to have developed a rather complex set of moral dispositions and opinions. How does this process of socialization and moralization take place? A developing morality in a child may undergo changes in all of the dimensions already discussed—in specific content, in mode of justification, and in degree of rationality—plus many other sorts of changes as well. Any attempt to understand and characterize the institution of morality will be handicapped if there is no awareness of the kinds of changes that typically occur in the development of a morality.

The development of morality *within a group or culture* has drawn considerable attention from social anthropologists.[16] So far as inquiry into moral development *within the individual* is concerned, if we construe this inquiry as inquiry into the techniques by which a child may be educated into a particular set of moral values, then the topic has received almost unlimited attention since the beginning of human history. Every culture has a stake in the inculcation of a set of moral values into its young; and nearly every parent faces the problem of how to go about this inculcation. But if the inquiry into how moral development in the child occurs is to be understood as itself free of any particular commitment to what is right and good; if it concerns itself with such matters as a comparison of the moral development of children from various cultures with differing moralities; if it is to be an empirical study for the social scientist, and not an attempt to establish guidelines for the moral propagandist, then the inquiry into moral development has received relatively less attention. Pioneering work on the subject was done by Jean Piaget.[17] More recently, substantial contributions have been made by Lawrence Kohlberg.[18] But whereas Piaget's theorizing was based upon relatively meager data, Kohlberg's results are grounded in fairly extensive and sound empirical research, and he has, therefore, been able to provide empirical tests for many of Piaget's hypotheses. I will therefore limit my attention to a brief summary of the relevant aspects of Kohlberg's results.

Studies of the moral development of young men of various class levels in Taiwan, Yucatan, Turkey, and the United States were initiated several years ago and are still being carried out. As a result of these studies, Kohlberg concludes that six distinct stages of moral development may be discerned, stages that "appear to be culturally universal."[19] These stages have the following characteristics: a) They concern only the form or structure of a morality, leaving open the question of its specific content; b) they are strictly sequential. For instance, Stage Four is never attained without first passing through Stages One, Two, and Three;[20] c) completion of the sequence is not universal. Many individuals, and perhaps all individuals in some cultures, never attain to the higher stages; d) The responses of most individuals constitute a mixture of stages—say, of Three, Four, and Five—so that classification of a particular case is usually only approximate.

Kohlberg's six stages, which he divides into three "levels," are as follows:

Level I: "Premoral" (or "Preconventional")

Stage 1: Orientation toward punishment and unquestioning deference to superior power. The physical consequences of action regardless of their human meaning or value determine its goodness or badness.

Stage 2: Right action consists of that which instrumentally satisfies one's own needs and occasionally the needs of others. Human relations are viewed in terms like those of the marketplace. Elements of fairness, of reciprocity and equal sharing are present, but they are always interpreted in a physical, pragmatic way. Reciprocity is a matter of "you scratch my back and I'll scratch yours" not of loyalty, gratitude or justice.

Level II: "Morality of conventional role conformity"

Stage 3: Good-boy-good-girl orientation. Good behavior is that which pleases or helps others and is approved by them. There is much conformity to stereotypical images of what is majority or "natural" behavior. Behavior is often judged by intention—"he means well" becomes important for the first time, and is overused, as by Charlie Brown in *Peanuts*. One seeks approval by being "nice."

Stage 4: Orientation toward authority, fixed rules and the maintenance of the social order. Right behavior consists of doing one's duty, showing respect for authority and maintaining the given social order for its own sake. One earns respect by performing dutifully.

Level III: "Morality of self-accepted moral principles" (or "postconventional")

Stage 5: A social-contract orientation, generally with legalistic and utilitarian overtones. Right action tends to be defined in terms of general rights and in terms of standards which have been critically examined and agreed upon by the whole society. There is a clear awareness of the relativism of personal values and opinions and a corresponding emphasis upon procedural rules for reaching consensus. Aside from what is constitutionally and democratically agreed upon, right or wrong is a matter of personal "values" and "opinion." The result is an emphasis upon the possibility of *changing* law in terms of rational considerations of social utility, rather than freezing it in the terms of Stage 4 "law and order." Outside of the legal realm, free agreement and contract are the binding elements of obligation. This is the "official" morality of American government, and finds its ground in the thought of the writers of the Constitution.

Stage 6: Orientation toward the decisions of conscience and toward self-chosen *ethical principles* appealing to logical comprehensiveness, universality and consistency. These principles are abstract and ethical (the Golden Rule, the categorical imperative); they are not concrete moral rules like the Ten Commandments. Instead, they are universal principles of *justice,* of the *reciprocity* and *equality* of human rights, and of respect for the dignity of human beings as *individual persons.*[21]

Kohlberg has distinguished some 32 "aspects" of morality and has characterized the six stages by their varying stances with respect to each of these aspects. For instance, regarding the "motivation for rule obedience or moral action," the six stages manifest themselves as follows:

Stage 1. Obey rules to avoid punishment.
Stage 2. Conform to obtain rewards, have favors returned, and so on.
Stage 3. Conform to avoid disapproval, dislike by others.
Stage 4. Conform to avoid censure by legitimate authorities and resultant guilt.
Stage 5. Conform to maintain the respect of the impartial spectator judging in terms of community welfare.
Stage 6. Conform to avoid self-condemnation.[22]

If they are as sound as they appear to be, Kohlberg's results are indeed impressive. For our purposes, however, it is fortunately not necessary to give a detailed appraisal of his contentions. Whether or not his six stages have the degree of cultural universality that he claims for them, they are in any case all recognizable as possible stages in the development of a morality; furthermore, a little observation and reflection will confirm the claim that they represent at least a very familiar and common sequence in the lives of individuals. Kohlberg's

clear delineation of the six stages casts additional light
upon some matters discussed earlier, and inspires other,
additional insights as well.

For instance, in discussing the notion of visceral morality as natural good health, I came to the conclusion
that a necessary condition for having a morality was possession of at least some disposition or motivation to act
out of a sense of the good and the right, where *good* and
right were not construed simply as names for what one
feels inclined to do or finds prudent to do. Kohlberg's
labeling of Stages One and Two as "premoral" is consistent with this claim, for motivation at these earlier stages
appears to be purely hedonistic or prudential. Only at
the later stages does there develop a sense of what is
right and good that is to some degree independent of
personal consequences that the agent may expect to experience as a result of his own actions.

The six stages in "motivation for rule obedience or
moral action" (cited above) are characterized by Kohlberg as "successive degrees of internalization of moral
sanctions."[23] And this concept of internalization (which I
have already appealed to in a vague sort of way) is at the
center of recent discussions of morality in the literature
of psychology.[24] Kohlberg defines internalization as
"learning to conform to rules in situations that arouse
impulses to transgress and that lack surveillance and
sanctions."[25] Kohlberg is only echoing a widespread
(though not universal) point of view when he understands the study of moral development itself as essentially the study of internalization.

Kohlberg's results shed new light on an old debate
concerning the role of the individual versus the role of a
group or culture in the formation of a morality. Traditional utilitarians and others tended to see morality as

arising out of the way in which a rational, autonomous individual perceived the requirements of social interaction. Recent work in social anthropology— that of Emile Durkheim, in particular—has emphasized rather the supremacy of custom and group mores in maintaining a morality, with individual morality being dominated by sheer respect for tradition and group authority. Kohlberg's studies suggest that both analyses of morality are correct, when applied to different stages of the moral development of the individual. In his own words,

> Moral judgment and emotion based on respect for custom, authority, and the group are seen as one phase or stage in the moral development of the individual rather than as the total definition of the essential characteristics it was for Durkheim. Judgment of right and wrong in terms of the individual's consideration of social-welfare consequences, universal principles, and justice is seen as a later phase of development. (p. 487)

Such a conclusion serves to underline the complexity of morality, and the difficulties facing any attempt to characterize it in a comprehensive way. Kohlberg's delineation of the various stages of moral development may also help to clarify certain controversies in recent moral philosophy. Insofar as ethics is construed as a normative discipline, seeking to establish acceptable moral rules, standards, and ideals, it is essentially an outgrowth of Level III, the postconventional or autonomous level, of moral development. Some philosophers define moral philosophy in essentially these terms.[26] But recent moral philosophy has also been motivated by the desire to understand and describe moral concepts and moral reasoning, without attempting to establish any normative conclusions, and this latter enterprise has, I suggest, often turned its attention upon morality as it occurs at earlier stages than those of Level III. May not, for instance, some of the controversy between the emotivists and their critics be seen as the result of focusing upon different levels of moral development? As I argued above, emotivism has some plausibility as a description of a significant portion of the morally sensitive public, but is less plausible as an account of another segment whose moral codes are expressed in a relatively rational way.

What lessons for our analysis of morality are we to draw from Kohlberg's results? Ideally, a definition of morality would be such as to include Stages Three through Six of moral development as delineated by him. But the radical variety of ways in which morality may be manifested as it develops in the individual poses significant problems for any attempt to provide a general definition of morality. As I have stated earlier, my chief concern is for the relationship between the concept of morality and concepts such as utility, benefit, social welfare, and related ideas. Now, the person who wishes to argue for an analytic connection between these two sets of concepts may find some support in the description of Stages Three through Five, but there appears to be some difficulty with his claim when it is confronted with the fact of Stage Six. In chapter 5 I will suggest that the flexibility of the concept of morality (which is here evidenced by Kohlberg's stages of moral development) rules out the feasibility of a definition of morality in terms of satisfaction of interest, social harmony, and so on.

Scope of the Moral Community

In every morality there will be some sort of conception of who or what counts as worthy of moral concern, and there will be some sort of conception of who or what participates, or is morally responsible and answerable for his actions. Thus we think of infants as having interests and rights that require to be taken into consideration in moral deliberation, but we generally do not think of them as moral participants or moral agents, capable of responsible behavior and subject to moral restraints. Healthy adults, on the other hand, are generally regarded both as deserving of moral concern and as capable of being moral agents. I will refer to these two dimensions of a morality as its *scope of moral concern* and its *scope of moral participants*.[27]

Variations in both of these dimensions are readily apparent when one surveys various moral systems. The scope of moral concern in some moralities (such as that of Hinduism, for example) may extend to all living things, or even perhaps beyond the category of life itself. In other moralities, especially the moralities of certain preliterate cultures, moral concern extends only to members of the immediate cultural group to which one belongs, and no further. Men of other tribes, even if they are recognized to be biologically indistinguishable from oneself, may be regarded as deserving of no greater moral consideration than animals that are slaughtered for one's personal needs. Variations in the scope of moral concern are usually to be found even within a single cultural group. We frequently, for instance, encounter disagreement concerning the degree to which the welfare of animals should figure in our moral deliberations. Opinions also differ as to whether the interests of future unborn generations deserve to be considered in moral deliberation.

Furthermore, within the scope of moral concern there typically are to be found gradations of concern. The average morally sensitive adult feels more moral concern for his family than for mere acquaintances, and more for acquaintances than for total strangers. When the object of moral concern is a person who lives at a great distance, in a radically different culture, the degree of moral concern may approach zero.

But a confusion may arise here that it is advisable to dispel. The scope of moral concern should be distinguished from what might be called the *scope of accepted responsibility*. This latter scope concerns the range in which an individual (or a group) regards himself (or itself) as having assignable moral responsibilties. Thus a person may regard victims of a famine in India as deserving of moral concern, yet regard himself as so situated that he can have no moral responsibility for these victims. The victims in India fall within the scope of his moral concern, but not within the scope of his accepted responsibility. It is often the case that what appear to be limitations on the scope of a person's moral concern are in reality limitations upon the scope of what he accepts as his specific responsibility. But even discounting variations in scope of accepted responsibility, there remain great variations in the scope of moral concern, from person to person and from group to group.

As for the scope of moral participants, there are several ways in which differences may arise. At what age do children become morally responsible? Is any form of mental illness grounds for excusing a man's behavior? If not, then what varieties and degrees of mental illness (if any) count as excusing conditions? Are alcoholics, or drug addicts, morally responsible for their behavior? Answers to these and similar questions vary widely from one morality to another.

The scope of moral participants is as a rule included

within, and smaller than, the scope of moral concern. But there would appear to be at least the logical possibility that a person might be regarded as a moral agent while being outside the scope of moral concern. Such a person would be held to be morally answerable for his behavior, and subject to moral obligations, yet not deserving of consideration in any moral deliberations. Certain elitist, inhuman moralities perhaps approach such a conception. Still, conceptions of the scope of moral participants are generally such that anything that falls outside the scope of moral concern is not considered to be a moral agent.

How are these matters relevant to an analysis of the concept of morality? Their chief significance lies in how they bear upon discussions of generality, objectivity, universality, universalizability, and other related notions, discussions that have been prominent in recent moral philosophy. I hope to skirt most of the thornier problems to be found here, but I cannot ignore the matter entirely. At this point I will offer only a few, preliminary remarks.

One conclusion is immediately apparent: if we may use the term as we did above, then it cannot be a necessary part of the concept of morality that any morality must regard all of humanity as deserving of moral concern. For, as noted, there exist many codes that it seems reasonable to call moral codes but that display no moral concern for all men as such, and in general. In this respect, morality is not by definition universal.

Shall we simply refuse to call anything a morality if it is not universal in its scope of concern? Ordinary usage may sometimes support such a limitation, but probably more frequently does not. Certainly the literature of psychology, sociology, and anthropology clearly countenances a conception of morality that admits nonuniversal codes.

A consequence of the restriction of the term *morality* to codes that are universal in their scope of concern is that only a minority of people in man's history may then be said to have adhered to a morality of any kind, for the evidence suggests that adherence to a genuinely universal code has been more the exception than the rule.

Furthermore, the notion of a universal code becomes itself unclear when one reflects that the scope of concern of a code frequently extends beyond humanity itself, to animals and even sometimes to plants. A Hindu may reasonably claim greater universality for his scope of concern than may a man for whom only humans count. What, then, is "genuine" universality in scope of concern?

Should we say, then, that although the scope of moral *concern* may vary widely in genuine moralities, it is nevertheless a logical requirement of moralities that the principles and rules that they espouse be *binding upon all men?* That, in short, the scope of moral *participants* be in some sense universal? But there are serious difficulties with this suggestion as well. In the first place, it was noted above that the scope of moral participants is generally limited to a subclass of the scope of moral concern. It follows that any code that is nonuniversal in scope of concern is almost certain to be nonuniversal in scope of participants as well. Must humans who fall outside the scope of moral concern be nevertheless thought of as responsible moral agents, in order for a code to count as a morality? If moralities may be nonuniversal in their scope of concern, it hardly seems reasonable to insist that they must by definition be universal in their scope of participants.

Second, the notion of universality is unclear here as it was above. What does universality in scope of moral participants mean, in the face of all of the possible gradations from infant to adult and psychotic to sane man? Is a morality that regards schizophrenics as morally responsible agents a more universal morality than one that does not? Is such a code a *more genuine* morality, or a *morally better* morality, by virtue of its wider scope? The answer to these questions is surely *no*.

I conclude that an analysis of *moral*$_1$ will not, by itself, determine the scope of moral concern or the scope of moral participants. How these latter are specified is itself largely a moral problem, that is, a problem concerning the proper content of *moral*$_2$.[28]

This brief discussion of universality in morality has, of course, left many related questions untouched. One may grant what is claimed above, yet nevertheless insist that generalization, in some form, is a necessary characteristic of moral judgments. One such position—a promising one, in fact—is that although moral judgments are not necessarily made "for all men," they are necessarily made *for all moral agents,* that is, for all things falling within one's scope of moral participants, even if these participants be only members of one's tribe. It might be further contended—although this claim is more controversial—that in any genuine morality, the scopes of moral concern and moral participants must be defined without using "egocentric particulars" or proper names. These are very difficult claims to sort out and appraise, and I leave them for the time being.

Stringency of Moral Principles

Another important dimension of variation is variation

in the *stringency* or *force* of moral "oughts."[29] The degree to which a moral requirement is regarded as binding, and the severity with which a breach of the requirement is viewed, obviously vary quite considerably. If a man has an impulse to murder another person, he ought to control that impulse; and if a man has promised to send an occasional postcard to his parents while he is vacationing, he ought to do so. But the first ought is, at least from our point of view, far more important and morally binding than the second.

Variation in degree of stringency or force of moral oughts is especially important when we come to consider the popular claim that, in order for something to count as a moral principle, it must be regarded as "overriding," or "supreme," or "superior" to other principles. There is considerable plausibility to assertions of this kind. Does not a moral obligation take precedence over a counsel of prudence, or a recommendation regarding etiquette? But the claim is capable of various interpretations, at least some of which have serious difficulties. Are moral oughts by definition more stringent or binding than nonmoral oughts? If so, how are we to accommodate the fact of variations in degree of stringency among moral oughts themselves, and the corollary fact that some moral oughts properly take precedence over others? Where is the cut-off point between moral and nonmoral oughts, in degree of stringency? Is it never the case that a nonmoral ought *legitimately* takes precedence over a moral ought? (Could not, for instance, a directive concerning a matter of very considerable aesthetic importance properly take precedence over a mild moral obligation?) I leave these questions without attempting to answer them here.

Type and Severity of Sanctions

Another way in which moralities may differ is in the sanctions that are favored in their support. Some cultures favor a severe, aggressive response to breaches of morality; others are far more subtle and restrained in their responses. What may be regarded in one society as a severe, harsh social sanction may in another be regarded as a mere "slap on the wrist." Within a given culture, the severity of sanctions for moral transgressions is in most cases loosely related to the importance with which the violated rule is regarded. But this relationship is not a simple one; the severity of sanctions that are favored or actually applied is not a direct function of the degree of importance attached to the rule that has been violated. It is possible, in fact, for a person to hold a moral principle, yet for various reasons not favor any form of punishment in response to breaches of it. The two questions "Is X guilty of a moral transgression?" and "Should X be punished in any way for his behavior?" are logically distinct; and an affirmative response to the first question need not entail an affirmative response to the second.[30] There may be moral transgressions that one cannot do much about; and there may be moral transgressions where sanctions *could* be applied but are not, for the reason that application of sanctions would have no utilitarian value.

These remarks take on special importance in view of a fairly widespread supposition that moral principles may be uniquely distinguished by the degree and kind of sanctions that are favored in their support.[31] The variability of sanctions noted in the preceding paragraph casts doubt on such a claim. It is in fact the case that if a person adheres to a moral principle of some sort, he is likely to favor some sort of social sanctions in support of that principle; but the correlation is not a very reliable one. Some further attention will be given to this matter later, when we come to the relationship between the concept of morality and the notion of social utility.

Review

I have noted and discussed the following dimensions of variation in morality: specific content, character of more general principles appealed to, degree of rationality, plus an extended discussion of nonrational morality; levels of moral development in the individual, scope of the moral community, the stringency of moral oughts, and variety in moral sanctions. There are many other ways in which moralities may vary, but the above are of chief importance for our purposes. As I attempt in later chapters to analyze the notion of morality, this review and discussion of variations should serve as a useful conceptual backdrop—exercising some control over the direction of the inquiry, enlightening that inquiry with an awareness of the diversity of moral phenomena, and thereby helping to forestall an overly narrow definition of the concept of morality.

1. In his excellent essay "On the Diversity of Morals" in *Essays in Sociology and Social Philosophy* (London: William Heinemann, Ltd., 1956), 1: 97-129, Morris Ginsberg specifies and discusses several modes of variation in moralities. He has a different end in mind from mine, and the modes of variation he cites only partially overlap with those I mention and discuss in this chapter.

2. After several decades in which it was apparently taken for granted in sociological and anthropological circles that there were no such moral invariants, the question seems again to be an open one, with several reputable social scientists claiming to find moral universals of a very general sort. See for instance Ralph Linton, "Universal Ethical Principles: An Anthropological View," in *Moral Principles of Action*, ed. Ruth Nanda Anshen (New York: Harper and Bros., 1952), pp. 645-60; Morris Ginsberg, "On the Diversity of

Morals"; Clyde Kluckhohn, "Ethical Relativity: Sic et Non," *Journal of Philosophy*, 52 (1955): 663-77; May and Abraham Edel, *Anthropology and Ethics: The Quest for Moral Understanding*, especially chapter 3.

3. See especially R. B. Perry, *Realm of Value*, excerpt printed in *Problems of Moral Philosophy*, ed. Paul Taylor (Belmont, Calif.: Dickenson Publishing Co., Inc., 1967), pp. 20-24; S. Toulmin, *The Place of Reason in Ethics* (Cambridge: Cambridge University Press, 1961), p. 145; W. K. Frankena, "Recent Conceptions of Morality," in *Morality and the Language of Conduct*, ed. H. N. Castaneda and G. Nakhnikian (Detroit, Mich.: Wayne State University Press, 1965), pp. 1-21; also W. K. Frankena, "The Concept of Morality," *Journal of Philosophy* 63, no. 21 (Nov. 10, 1966): 688-96.

4. The problem remains, of course, how one is to distinguish between *moral* emotive reactions, and *nonmoral* emotive reactions such as simple anger, vindictiveness, love, or pleasure. Early emotive theories tended, in my opinion, not to provide a way of making this distinction. The consequence, which is hardly acceptable, is that any favorable or unfavorable emotive reaction to a person, action, etc., becomes a moral reaction. Our problem is to preserve the distinction between moral and nonmoral sentiments while still recognizing the possibility of a nonrational morality. Any satisfactory definition of morality must pass this test.

5. But see above, n4. See also chapter 1, section 3.

6. From *Diagnostic and Statistical Manual, Mental Disorders*, of the American Psychiatric Association, quoted by Hervey M. Cleckley, "Psychopathic Personality," *International Encyclopedia of the Social Sciences* (New York: Macmillan, 1968), 13: 113.

7. Cleckley, "Psychopathic Personality," p. 114.

8. *Ibid.*, p. 116.

9. *Ibid.*, p. 113.

10. This distinction closely parallels the famous Kantian distinction between acting *in accordance with duty* and acting *for the sake of duty*. See *Groundwork of the Metaphysics of Morals*, chapter (or section) 1, the "First Proposition" of morality. But Kant then proceeds to build upon this distinction as a basis for a normative theory of morality; he is ultimately concerned to provide a criterion for distinguishing the moral from the *im*moral. My purpose is, rather, to distinguish the moral from the *non*moral.

11. Although correct as it stands, this statement advances us not very far toward an analysis of the concept of morality. For a) *good* and *right* are, of course, terms that are not limited to moral contexts, but apply throughout practically all normative discourse; and b) insofar as we understand the terms in a *moral* sense, the statement is circular, taken as a definition of morality. At best, it is an illuminating tautology.

12. Jonathan Harrison, "When Is a Principle a Moral Principle?," *Proceedings of the Aristotelian Society*, 28 (suppl.) (1954): 113. See also the entry under "Morals," *Encyclopaedia of the Social Sciences* (New York: Macmillan, 1933), 10, esp. 646: it is claimed that moral experience is "compulsive, the feeling . . . of conformation to force."

13. Henry W. Brosin, "Obsessive-Compulsive Disorders," *International Encyclopedia of the Social Sciences* (1968), p. 241.

14. *Ibid.*

15. Provided, that is, that the notion of a *basic moral reaction* is construed broadly enough to encompass highly intellectualized, rational moral codes such as those referred to above.

16. The classical study on this topic is Leonard T. Hobhouse, *Morals in Evolution: A Study in Comparative Ethics* 7th ed. (London: Chapman, 1951). First published in 1906.

17. Jean Piaget, *The Moral Judgment of the Child* (Glencoe, Ill.: Free Press, 1948). First published in French in 1932.

18. For a summary of Kohlberg's results, see his article "Moral Development," *International Encyclopedia of the Social Sciences* (1968). 10: 483-93. See also Kohlberg, "The Child as Moral Philosopher," *Psychology Today* 2, no. 4 (Sept. 1968): 25-30.

19. Kohlberg, "Moral Development," p. 490.

20. Kohlberg expresses some doubts about this point in the case of the final two stages, leaving open the possibility that Stage Six may occur without being preceded by Stage Five. "The Child," p. 28.

21. Kohlberg, "The Child," p. 26. See also *idem*, "Moral Development," pp. 489-90.

22. Kohlberg, "Moral Development," p. 489.

23. *Ibid.*

24. *Ibid.*, p. 483.

25. *Ibid.*

26. See for example William K. Frankena, *Ethics* (Englewood Cliffs, N.J.: Prentice Hall Foundations of Philosophy Series, 1963), pp. 3f.

27. This distinction is clearly made, using somewhat different terminology, in Edel, *Anthropology and Ethics*, p. 86.

28. I do not wish to deny that there may be *some* logical limitations on what could possibly count as a moral agent or an object of moral concern. I would suppose, for instance, that inanimate objects (when thought of as inanimate objects rather than as, say, disguised personalities or spirits) could not without logical contradiction come under the scope of *moral* participants, in a morality. I wish only to maintain that a) analysis of the concept of morality does not precisely specify the scopes of moral concern and moral participants; and b) in particular, it leaves open the question of the degree of universality of these scopes.

29. Many authors, in place of phrases like *moral requirement* or the awkward *moral ought* would use the phrase *moral obligation*. The notion of obligation seems however, to characterize only a portion of judgments concerning moral rightness. Not every moral "ought" is a moral obligation.

30. For this way of putting the distinction, I am indebted to Professor Roderick Firth.

31. For a fully developed statement of the position that the type of supporting sanctions determines whether or not a principle counts as a moral principle, see Timothy Sprigge, "Definition of a Moral Judgment," *Philosophy* 39 (1964): 301-22. See also J. S. Mill, *Utilitarianism*, ed. Oskar Piest (Library of Liberal Arts, 1957), pp. 60f. Use of a sanction criterion to differentiate moral from nonmoral codes has been fairly common in anthropological circles. For a classical statement by an anthropologist on the subject of sanctions, see A. R. Radcliffe-Brown, "Social Sanctions," *Encyclopedia of the Social Sciences* (1934), 13: 531-34, especially p. 531.

3
Reflections in Midstream

Before proceeding further, it may be worthwhile to pause, look back, and consider our progress to date, as well as to counter some possible criticisms that may have accumulated along the way. In the light of our preanalytic notions of morality, and in view of what has already been said in the first two chapters, is it possible to arrive at some preliminary delimitations of the concept of morality? Certain remarks may be made at this stage.

Morality and Right Conduct

For a start, it seems reasonable to insist that anything that is to count as a morality must, at least in part, have to do with conduct. More specifically: in order for something to be a morality, it must *serve to direct and assess conduct.* A "morality" that does not in any way help to answer the questions "What should I (or he, they, etc.) do?" and "What should I (or he, they, etc.) have done?" is not a morality at all. That moralities must deal with conduct is hardly a controversial claim; indeed, the characteristic is one that is generally mentioned in dictionary definitions of morality. It seems to me to be sufficiently obvious not to require further defense here.

Further Preliminary Parameters

Are we in a position to lay down any further, more substantial limits to the application of the term *morality*? May and Abraham Edel, who caution against overly narrow definitions of morality, and who employ the term in a very flexible and extensive way, nevertheless cite a number of structural characteristics that they apparently regard as common to all moral systems:

> each code involves honorable behavior, orderly and sometimes sensitive behavior, concerned with doing right according to some accepted standards, and judging others by the same code; it involves approved traits of character, virtues and vices, as well as rules of good and bad behavior, and ideas concerning the whys and wherefores of at least some of the principles involved. There is often considerable group involvement in maintaining the code, including educating children in conformity with it, and treating conformists and offenders with required degrees of reward, punishment, social praise or blame.[1]

The Edels seem to be thinking here of naturally evolved moralities of various cultural groups, moralities of the kind that are of interest to the anthropologist. When one considers the range of all possible moralities, including unusual and eccentric moralities of individuals, perhaps not everything mentioned in the above quotation will apply. For instance, if what was said in chapter 2 concerning the possibility of nonrational, "visceral" moralities is correct, then it is not the case that every morality must contain "ideas concerning the whys and wherefores of at least some of the principles involved." And in their observation that "There is *often* [my emphasis] considerable group involvement in maintaining the code . . . ," the Edels appear to recognize that

variations in social sanctions occur, and that "group involvement" is not universal to all moralities.

But after such allowances are made, some structural
constants remain, and may be distilled from the passage.
They are as follows:

1) Every morality contains "rules of good and bad behavior." (This characteristic has already been provided for by the requirement that moralities direct
   and appraise conduct.)
2) Every morality involves some notion of what is honorable, and some notion of "approved traits of
   character."
3) Every morality appraises in the light of standards that
   are regarded as more than purely private; it is concerned with "judging others by the same code" that
   one applies to oneself.

These three sets of characteristics, while perhaps not
advancing us very far, nevertheless appear to me to be
necessary to anything that could properly be called a
morality. In the spectrum of moralities reviewed in
chapter 2, no instance of a morality was described in
such a way as to lack any of these characteristics; and if
any code of value failed to exhibit them, I should be reluctant to call it a morality. But let us consider them in
more detail.

Since I have already briefly discussed the first requirement, I pass over it here. But the second has not
been treated before, and merits some closer attention.
The first observation to make is that as they are most
frequently used, the terms *honorable* and *good character*
are *already moral terms*. To describe a man as honorable,
or to say that he is a man of good character, is tan-

tamount to saying that he *is governed by dispositions to be-*
have in morally correct or admirable ways; that in general he
can be counted upon to behave in a moral$_2$ fashion, and
perhaps that he has a record of moral$_2$ behavior in the
past. If in defining the terms *honorable* and *good character*
we must appeal to the concept of morality itself, then to
cite notions of honor and good character as characteristics of a morality does not advance us very far in our
analysis. To expand on this point:

Of a fine creative artist, a man who has produced excellent works of art and who has dispositions to behave
in aesthetically admirable ways, we would not automatically say that he was a man "of good character." Of a
fine logician and man of rational intellect, we would not
automatically say that he was a man "of good character."
We should apply this phrase to the two men only after
determining that they displayed fine *moral* qualities, and
not merely fine aesthetic and intellectual qualities. It is
tautologous to say "A man of good character is a morally
good man." Referral questionnaires that ask about a
man's character wish to know about his moral qualities.

In general, similar remarks hold for the notion of an
honorable man (although *honor* perhaps picks out a
more specific set of moral qualities than does *good
character*).[2]

There is, however, some slight conceptual advance in
the observation that a morality must contain notions of
honorable traits and good character, for this observation
highlights the importance to morality of the *appraisal of
dispositions.* A morality cannot be merely a set of directives for and appraisals of conduct alone; it must also
engage in the appraisal of dispositions to behave in various ways.

To make this point more valid, consider a hypothetical

code of value that prescribed and evaluated only specific human actions and types of behavior, and no more. Such a code would allow us to say that a man did a good thing, but it would not allow us to say that a man was a good man. Or, at most, a *good man* would mean a "man who happens to have committed good acts." Since the dispositions that give rise to behavior would not themselves be evaluated, good and bad actions would appear as coincidences of value against a value-neutral background. Moral evaluation of *persons,* as we understand it, would not occur; and the whole gamut of ordinary moral virtues and vices would either be absent, or else present only in a radically different form. Although such a code of value might have significant analogies to a moral code, it would not, I suggest, count as a genuine morality. A morality must not only direct and appraise behavior; it must also evaluate traits or dispositions to behave.

As for the third characteristic cited above, it in effect introduces the notion of generalization in ethics; for it specifies that a morality must be evaluated in the light of standards that are held to be interpersonal. A morality cannot be a set of rules that are rules just "for me" or just "for you"; they must in some sense be rules "for anyone"—perhaps "for anyone within the scope of moral participants." I think that some sort of criterion of generalization is indeed required; but the precise form that it should take is very difficult to determine, and I again defer the matter. In chapter 4 I will have some suggestions to make regarding it.

To summarize our results to date:

1) A morality serves to direct and appraise conduct; it contains rules of right and wrong behavior.

2) A morality serves to appraise dispositions to behave; it contains notions of good and bad personal traits.

3) A morality appeals to rules and standards that are thought of as general and interpersonal, in some as yet unspecified sense.

4) Having a morality involves having at least some disposition to judge and act out of what one feels to be good and right, where *good* and *right* are not simply other names for what one feels personally inclined to do, or finds prudent to do.[3]

These criteria are not themselves sufficient to separate moral evaluation from other types of evaluation. For instance, provided that the terms *good* and *right* in the above criteria are construed broadly enough so as not to be question-begging, the four criteria together are broad enough to admit evaluation not only in terms or moral norms, but in terms of aesthetic norms and intellectual or "logical" norms as well. Thus, imagine that a music critic is evaluating a particular pianist as a performing artist. He may 1) evaluate the pianist's performance (i.e., his conduct) as good or bad, and 2) see this performance as indicative of personal traits that are, aesthetically speaking, good or bad traits for an artist to have. In making his evaluation, the critic may 3) appeal to norms of excellence that he thinks of as appropriate for any person who finds himself in the role of a pianist. And 4) the critic's sense of the aesthetically right and good may run counter to his personal inclinations and prudential calculations. For instance, the critic may have a personal liking for the pianist and therefore wish to comment favorably on the performance, yet be compelled by his sense of aesthetic value to comment unfavorably. And this same sense of aesthetic value may compel the critic to take an unpopular stance that might be damaging to his personal career.

Similar remarks could be made for evaluation in terms of norms of good reasoning, and perhaps for evaluation of other kinds. Thus more must be said, if we are to differentiate moral evaluation from other kinds of evaluation, and thereby clarify the concept of a morality. But additional criteria of a morality should at least be consistent with the four given above.

Concluding Remarks

But what are these further criteria that are required to delimit the concept of morality in an appropriate way? It is, I believe, at this point that the philosophical endeavor to define morality begins to run afoul of the variation in acceptable usage of the term in ordinary discourse. In chapter 1 I noted the indefiniteness of the term *morality* in ordinary usage, and the tendency for one's conception of what is moral$_2$ to exercise some control over what one thinks could count as a possible morality. Because of this vagueness, I believe that it will be impossible to arrive at one clear conception of morality that captures all of the more or less correct uses of the term in ordinary language. If this point is correct, then any analysis of the concept must be to some degree reformatory or stipulative, if only in that it fastens upon a portion of ordinary usage and excludes another portion.

Even if one focuses upon logically central uses of the term *morality*, the "centric rather than eccentric" uses, and even if one keeps in mind as a guideline for analysis the functional and structural characteristic of moralities, it may well be that we cannot single out one decisive set of criteria for having a morality. For the concept may be such that there can be found only several competing criteria, a cluster of "morality-making" characteristics such that not every individual one of the cluster is absolutely necessary, and such that a number of possible subsets of the cluster are sufficient. And it is probably the case that what counts as a morality in some respects shades off evenly into what does not count as a morality. (Perhaps, for instance, the distinction between rules of morality and rules of etiquette is vague in this way.) If so, any analysis of morality should reflect such a vagueness of its boundaries.

1. May Edel and Abraham Edel, *Anthropology and Ethics: The Quest for Moral Understanding*, rev. ed. (Cleveland, Ohio: The Press of Case Western Reserve University, 1968), p. 15.

2. The adjective *honorable* is perhaps more closely tied to the concept of morality than is the corresponding noun, *honor*. A "code of honor" is not necessarily a morality; and to speak of "honor among thieves" is not necessarily to attribute a morality to them. Though thieves may adhere to a code of honor, to say this is not *ipso facto* to declare that they are honorable persons.

3. See chapter 2, "Morality as Natural Good Health."

4
Utility and Social Harmony: I

> Morality is man's endeavor to harmonize conflicting interests: to prevent conflict when it threatens, to remove conflict when it occurs, and to advance from the negative harmony of non-conflict to the positive harmony of cooperation.[1]
>
> —Ralph Barton Perry

> What makes us call a judgment "ethical" is the fact that it is used to harmonize people's actions . . .[2]
>
> —Stephen Toulmin

> . . . by the "moral point of view" we *mean* a point of view which furnishes a court of arbitration for conflicts of interests.[3]
>
> —Kurt Baier

> . . . some reference to the welfare of others, the security of social life, etc., is part of the meaning of words like "moral" and "morality" . . .[4]
>
> —William K. Frankena

The object of this chapter is twofold. The first general objective is to state and discuss several related criteria that have been offered as necessary conditions of any morality, and to distill out of these related criteria one criterion that combines the most promising aspects of each of the original versions. I call this criterion the *allocation criterion.* That the allocation criterion states a necessary condition for anything that is to count as a morality is, when examined, a highly plausible claim. The second general objective of this chapter is to exhibit that plausibility in some detail, by showing how the allocation criterion nicely accounts for several leading and highly typical features of morality. The discussion will hopefully help to explain why the allocation criterion, or something like it, has been regarded by a number of eminent moral philosophers as a necessary condition of a moral code. But whereas this chapter will give the allocation criterion a sympathetic hearing, chapter 5 will attempt to show that, despite its plausibility, the allocation criterion is *not* a necessary mark of the moral.

The Allocation Criterion

Every individual has interests—desires, impulses, inclinations, needs, goals, and so forth—of various kinds. Furthermore, individuals interact with one another in social settings, and in the course of this interaction, their respective interests frequently come into conflict or competition. That which promotes the satisfaction and welfare of one individual often does not promote the satisfaction and welfare of another. Some sort of organized system of rules governing the way men are to live together would seem to be required, if the conflict and competition of interests are not to erupt constantly into strife. All of these remarks are platitudinous. Is it not also a platitude, a truism, to say that a morality is essentially an organized system of rules of this kind? Are not various moralities simply various ways in which men

have responded to the need for some regularized allocation of advantages in possible conflict-of-interest situations?

To answer these questions affirmatively is to say that
moralities are, in effect, programs for social harmony,
intended to govern human interaction by agreement
rather than by hostilities. Perry's requirement (stated
above) that a morality must be in some sense an "endeavor to harmonize conflicting interests" is closely related, furthermore, to Frankena's requirement that a
morality must have "some reference to the welfare of
others, the security of social life, etc." In order to see
that this is so, it will be useful here to specify four alternative claims about the essential nature of morality and
to discuss their relations to each other. These claims are
as follows:

A) A morality necessarily prescribes and evaluates conduct at least partly in terms of *its effects upon people.*
B) A morality necessarily prescribes and evaluates conduct at least partly in terms of its *consequences for
   human welfare and benefit.*[5]
C) A morality necessarily is intended by its adherents *to
   promote some allocation of advantages in possible
   conflict-of-interest situations.*
D) A morality necessarily is intended by its adherents *to
   promote social harmony.*

Now, a philosopher who seriously urged requirement
A presumably would not intend to insist that a morality
must concern itself with *all* of the probable consequences
of conduct upon others. An action of mine may result in
the bouncing of a stray hydrogen atom off of the skin of
another person; yet that event would presumably not be

thought to have moral significance if it in no significant way affected the desires, inclinations, goals, needs, and so on—in short, the *interests*—of that person, or any other person. Philosophers who urge requirement A surely have in mind, therefore, something like the following:

(A1) A morality necessarily prescribes and evaluates conduct at least partly in terms of *its effects upon the satisfaction of interests of people.*

Does this interpretation of A show it to be identical with B? Not entirely; for the notion of satisfaction of interest, in the broad sense in which I use it here, is not identical with the notions of welfare or benefit as they are usually understood. What satisfies some of a person's interests is not necessarily to his benefit, as any victim of overeating can testify. Still, if the notion of a person's interest is to include long-range interests, "overall" interests, reflective, rationally considered interests, and so on, then the notions of welfare or benefit would seem to be included in the notion of satisfaction of interest.

To elaborate: In the broad sense in which I use the concept of interest, a person may be said to have an interest in something without having an identifiable desire for that thing, provided that the thing (state, effect, result, etc.) in fact would, on balance, *conduce to the satisfaction* of the person. Thus a person may be said to have an interest in something provided that a) he has an identifiable desire for that thing, or b) he *would* have a desire for that thing if he were *rational, well-informed,* and *motivated to maximize his own satisfaction.* To cite an example of the latter kind of interest: a person may, through ignorance, fail to realize that he has an interest in acquiring a high school diploma; put another way, he may fail to realize that it is *in his interest* to acquire a high school diploma. Now, saying that something is in the interest of a person is, according to common usage, roughly equivalent to saying that the thing is *to his benefit,* or *conduces to his welfare.*

On the other hand, I do not mean to use the concepts of interest, welfare, and benefit so broadly that anything that in *any* sense "makes a man better" or "improves a man" is *ipso facto* to his benefit or welfare, or is in his interest. Sometimes becoming a better man, or improving oneself—according, for instance, to some standard of morality, or aesthetics, or law—may, in a perfectly proper sense of the words, require that a man sacrifice his own welfare, curtail his interests, and abandon benefits to himself. Certainly it is not *analytically* true that to become a better man is always to benefit oneself, or to satisfy one's interests. To return to our notion of a rational, well-informed desire: we cannot simply assume that a man who was rational, well-informed, and motivated to maximize his own satisfaction would automatically desire to become a "better" man in every sense of the word, particularly if becoming better means improving oneself with regard to a given standard of aesthetic or moral value. There is no logical contradiction in saying that a man may sacrifice his own interests by behaving in a virtuous fashion.

Thus a man may be said to have an interest in something on numerous grounds. The thing in which he has an interest may be the object of a momentary desire—a whim or impulse; it may be the object of a rationally guided, long-range desire; or it may be something he *would* desire if he were rational, well-informed, and motivated to maximize his own satisfaction—even though he may *in fact* have no identifiable desire for it. It goes without saying that a man's interests may conflict with one another in a variety of ways.

I conclude that welfare or benefit may appropriately be considered to be *particular kinds* of satisfaction of interest, as I use this latter phrase. Requirement B is, therefore, if not identical with requirement A1, at least a special, narrower version of A1. Anything that met requirement B must meet requirement A1; and if one were to show that A1 does not state a necessary requirement of a morality, one would *a fortiori* have shown that B is not a necessary requirement. Consequently, I will concentrate upon the broader criterion, requirement A1, in my discussion.

What is the connection, if any, between A1 and C? They are, I think, much closer than they may appear at first. For: A1 requires of any morality that it prescribe conduct at least partly in terms of its effects upon the satisfaction of interests of people. Except for the case of pure egoism, briefly discussed below, prescriptions will thus concern themselves with the effects of one's conduct upon the satisfaction of interests of other persons. Now, any prescription or directive concerning how one *should* act is generally otiose and pointless except where one might conceivably *have an interest in behaving otherwise than as prescribed or directed.* It is where one might conceivably have an interest in disregarding the interests of others that prescriptions and directives concerning the interests of others have appropriate application. But this is to say that in such cases, one's interests and the interests of others are seen as in possible conflict with each other. In other words, *situations that are seen as involving possible conflicts of interest are the appropriate contexts for enjoinders to concern oneself with the interests and satisfactions of others.* Any body of value-beliefs and attitudes that gives rise to prescriptions for conduct on grounds of the effect of that conduct upon the satisfaction of interest of other persons must in effect seek to govern the allocation of advantages in at least some possible conflict-of-interest situations. Conversely, any prescription concerning how a conflict of interest should be resolved constitutes a prescription concerning the way in which interests should, or should not be, satisfied.[6]

There is a limiting case, the case of a purely egoistic system of value, in which a concern for the satisfaction of interest is only incidentally a concern for allocation of advantages in conflict-of-interest contexts. The pure egoist is concerned only to satisfy his own interests. In any conflict-of-interest situation, the only "allocation" he favors is the one in which all possible advantages accrue to himself. Such a person applies the terms *good* and *right* only to courses of action that he is inclined to do, or finds prudent to do, or that in some way conduce to his interest. But one of the typical marks of morality specified in chapter 3 excludes codes of behavior of this kind from the category of morality. I thus suggest that for all significant cases, requirements A1 and C come to essentially the same thing.

What, then, of requirement D? The phrase *social harmony* is, of course, vague. When given a minimal interpretation, however, I think D is simply an abbreviated, more colloquial version of C. According to that interpretation, social harmony results when conflicts of interest are either avoided or else resolved by some principles of allocation of advantages. Something like this understanding seems to be operative in the quotation from R. B. Perry that introduced this chapter. More elaborate and grandiose conceptions of social harmony are possible, and are often espoused as ethical or political ideals. In this chapter, however, I am concerned with the minimal conception, and will therefore understand D to be an abbreviated form of C.

The proposal to be discussed here is, then, the following: it is a necessary condition of any morality that it prescribe and evaluate conduct at least partly in terms of the expected consequences of that conduct for the satisfaction of human interests. An alternative formulation of the proposal is: it is a necessary condition of any morality that it be intended to promote some allocation of advantages in possible conflict-of-interest situations. These two formulations may be synthesized in the statement that any morality must be intended to promote some *allocation of interest-satisfaction*. I will refer to this joint formulation as the *allocation criterion*. Briefly and loosely put, the claim to be examined is that every morality must place a value of some kind on satisfaction of interest and social harmony.

In order to examine the plausibility of the allocation criterion, it will be useful to define another closely related concept, the concept of an *allocation issue*. As I employ the concept, to say that an allocation issue exists is to say that: a) there exist some (more than one) self-interested individuals, individuals who have various personal interests; b) these individuals have a stake in preserving or promoting a *social group* of which they personally are or shall be members; that is, they have a stake in preserving or promoting some degree of social interaction and cooperation with other self-interested persons; c) in the course of participation in the group, a conflict of interest between members of the group either has actually occurred or threatens to occur; d) thus, if a reasonable degree of social harmony is to prevail, some resolution of the actual or potential conflict is called for, by way of adjudication between competing interests and allocation of advantages among the persons whose interests are in conflict. In short, an allocation issue is a situation of possible or actual conflict of interest such that an allocation of advantages is required.

The relationship between the allocation criterion and allocation issues may be put in the following way: the allocation criterion was the requirement that every moral code concern itself at least partly with what is regarded as the proper resolution of allocation issues.

In addition to the allocation criterion and allocation issues, I shall speak of *allocation procedures*. Allocation procedures are to be understood as procedures that are employed for the purpose of dealing with and resolving allocation issues.

The Plausibility of the Allocation Criterion

The concepts of an allocation issue and an allocation procedure immediately suggest some observations that are relevant for our inquiry into the concept of morality. In the first place, we may note that any significant allocation issue is an issue that is, in an obvious sense, *socially important.* In an equally obvious sense, the allocation procedures that are employed within a group to deal with allocation issues are themselves socially important; and the principles or guidelines that govern allocation procedures are socially important principles or guidelines. The very notion of a society, as opposed to a mere collection of separate individuals, suggests some form of organization and some established procedures governing interaction and possible conflicts of interest. A society could hardly be said to exist unless there existed in it some more or less established allocation procedures for conflict-of-interest situations. To have some interest in the preservation of a society is to have some interest in the preservation of some procedures of this kind. It is to be expected, therefore, that the allocation procedures that a society in fact employs, and those which it might employ, will be matters of rather special concern to most members and participants in the society. Such procedures of the society will govern the way the members of the society are to live together and the way they are to treat each other. Allocation issues—issues that involve allocation of advantages in possible conflict-of-interest situations—are therefore likely to be thought of as issues of *special social importance.* They are likely to be thought of as issues that are *not purely the individual agent's own business,* but rather as issues *in which the community has a legitimate concern.*[7]

**Social Involvement and
Interference in
Moral Issues**

Now, beliefs of this kind—that an issue is of special social importance, and that how it is resolved is not merely the business of the individual, but also the legitimate concern of others in the group—are, I suggest, typically moral beliefs. When we know that a man has judged an action to be right (or wrong), we do not yet have good reason to conclude that he has made a moral judgment. But when we learn that he believes the issue about which he is judging to be of special social importance, and such that whether the action is done rightly is not merely the business of the agent but is also the legitimate concern of others, then we have, I suggest, rather strong (though not conclusive) evidence that he has made a moral judgment.

To be sure, the locutions *of special social importance* and *not merely the business of the agent but also the legitimate concern of others* are vague and call for further clarification. I will attempt to display their intuitive content by a preliminary example, and will then discuss the problem of how they are to be interpreted.

Suppose we overhear a man named Barnaby say to his acquaintance, Imhoff: "You know, you really ought to give your car a checkup before you take your trip." Under most circumstances we would probably take this judgment to be merely a bit of prudential advice, to the effect that Imhoff may well avoid some trouble and expense to himself if he gives his car a checkup. Suppose, however, that Imhoff's car is in rather bad shape, so that it may be dangerous to operate. Suppose that Imhoff is known to be irresponsible about such matters. Suppose that Imhoff plans to take a crowd of friends on the trip, whose welfare may be endangered by riding in the car. Suppose that Barnaby knows all of these things, and that in saying what he does, he takes the attitude that whether Imhoff gives the car a checkup is not merely Imhoff's business, but also the legitimate concern of the others who will be involved in the trip. Barnaby believes the matter to be not merely personally important (to Imhoff) but of some social importance as well. When we learn of these facts, I think we readily recognize Barnaby's judgment to be moral in force; the "ought" in his utterance is probably a *moral* ought.

This example clearly presents a case of an allocation issue. A conflict of interest is present, between Imhoff's inclination to be lazy and ignore the condition of the car, and the interests that those persons accompanying Imhoff have in avoiding inconvenience and bodily injury. The beliefs and attitudes of Barnaby are a natural reflection of this fact. We have, then, some initial corroboration for the claim that allocation issues naturally give rise to typically moral beliefs and attitudes.

It is time now to examine the way these beliefs and attitudes are described and to probe into their interpretation. When a person believes that an issue is "of special social importance" and "not merely the business of the individuals involved, but of legitimate concern to others as well," the most natural interpretation is that the person favors, at least under some conditions, a certain amount of *social interference* in the matter, as a means of insuring that the issue is resolved in what he regards as a satisfactory manner. It is natural, in short, to suppose that he favors the use of *social sanctions* of various kinds as a means of controlling the resolution of the issue. But if this is what the beliefs and attitudes come to, then it is clear that they do not always accompany moral judgments. For a man may regard an issue as a moral issue, yet *not* favor actual social interference in the matter. There may be a variety of reasons why the exercise of social control and the employment of social sanctions are not regarded as desirable. Perhaps there are supervening moral principles that make social meddling unacceptable in cases of a certain kind. Perhaps it is simply impractical, and would require too great an effort, to exert effective social influence. Perhaps the person holding the moral views is very tolerant or forgiving, and cannot bring himself to favor punishment as a response to moral misbehavior. Perhaps he holds beliefs of a fatalistic sort, to the effect that "people will do what they will do," regardless of the presence or absence of social sanctions. Perhaps he believes that how moral agents are to be treated for their obedience or disobedience to moral rules should be left to the discretion of a supreme being, and is not a matter in which humans should meddle.

Granting all of these cases as possibilities, we may still assert that the favoring of social sanctions in support of a rule or principle is a highly characteristic mark of moralities. It is so characteristic, in fact, that the criterion most commonly employed by anthropologists in identifying the moral dimension of a society is one that looks to the presence of social sanctions as the definitive feature of moral codes. According to A. MacBeath, a philosopher who has read widely in anthropological studies of cultural moral codes, a criterion in terms of social sanctions "is in fact the principle of division used by practically all anthropologists who deal with the subject."[8] A similar position has been attractive to several philosophers, including John Stuart Mill.[9] In a similar vein, it is sometimes asserted that what is distinctive about moral issues is that when they arise, the persons involved can no longer simply be left to their own devices and preferences. In matters of taste, *de gustibus non disputandum est.* But in matters of morality, it is said, *de gustibus* no longer holds. Men involved in moral issues are thought to be answerable to others in an especially strong sense; they can no longer be allowed to act simply as they please. If a man chooses to pour catsup over his hot fudge sundae, we may shudder at the sight, but allow him to do as he likes. But if he chooses to cheat the customers in his shop, or refuses employment to qualified blacks on the basis of race, we are prone to rise up in indignation and demand that measures be taken to discourage his objectionable behavior. Here, *de gustibus* does not apply; here, it is not simply his business how he behaves; here, the community may enter into the matter and exert influence upon his behavior.

All of these features that have been thought to be definitive of moral issues are features that fit naturally into the context of an allocation issue. Where a conflict of interest is present, and some adjudication of competing interests is called for if social harmony is to be preserved, it is natural to say that how a person behaves is no longer "his own business"; it is natural to hold individuals "answerable" to others; it is natural to favor that social sanctions be used, at least under some conditions, as a means of bringing about a resolution of the issue. I have suggested that these features do not universally accompany moral issues. Nevertheless, it has been popular to suppose that they *do* universally accompany moral issues; and the popularity of this supposition is nicely explained by the popularity of an underlying assumption that moral issues are necessarily allocation issues. In short, if we assume the allocation criterion to be a necessary mark of morality, then certain sorts of popular claims about what is typical or even definitive of morality are found to follow naturally upon that assumption. The supposition that the allocation criterion is necessary conforms nicely to certain widely held beliefs about morality.

To supplement and expand upon the above beginning, I will explore the notion of allocation issues further and will try to show that a number of concepts, attitudes, and judgments (beyond those already cited) that we think of as typically *moral* concepts, attitudes, and judgments are especially appropriate to these issues. What, then, are some of the more typical moral notions, and in what way are they "appropriate" in contexts where an allocation of interest-satisfaction is called for?

Self-Restraint and Egoism

Perhaps no notion is more closely associated with morality in the minds of ordinary individuals than the notion of self-control or self-restraint, in the face of impulses or inclinations that it is somehow desirable not to indulge. The curbing of "purely selfish" drives, and the control of private impulses and inclinations for the sake of some long-range or wider value—these are so characteristic of morality that some persons seem to regard self-control and self-sacrifice as the essence of morality. I venture to say that in no other area of value-theory is this feature, the demand for control of impulse and inclination, so prominent as it is in morality. In appraisal according to canons of good reasoning, and in aesthetic evaluation, it appears only in a limited way. Even in prudential judgments, which often enjoin control of present impulse for the sake of future good, the appeal is to one's own self-interest. On the other hand, it is typically thought that *moral* enjoinders and directives *frequently* and *characteristically* run counter not only to one's immediate impulses and inclinations, but also may run counter to one's personal long-range self-interest as well. As Baier says, "Moral directives must be regarded as capable of overriding not only inclination but also the directives of self-interest when a person cannot follow both. . . ."[10] Self-sacrifice is an almost exclusively *moral* virtue. And egoism, though it may subvert various goods, is thought to be *characteristically* subversive of moral goods.

Now, if the issues at stake are allocation issues, that is, if they are issues in which people are involved in a conflict of interests, and where some sort of adjudication between these competing interests—some allocation of advantages—is called for, then the prominence of the demand for self-control and self-sacrifice becomes eminently understandable. To say that a number of different interests are in conflict is presumably to say that not all interests can be fully satisfied simultaneously. It is to say that any adjudication of the conflict, any allocation of satisfaction of interest, will necessarily have the consequence that at least some parties to the conflict will have to forgo full satisfaction of their own interests. To favor any particular allocation is, therefore, in effect to call for some self-control and renunciation of personal interests on the part of at least some parties to the conflict. In some cases, the allocation called for will require that every party to the conflict sacrifice his personal interests to some degree. In a few cases, the allocation called for may require that some individuals sacrifice their personal interests completely, by giving up their lives.

In any case, a code of conduct that has to do essentially with adjudicating between conflicting interests is a code of conduct that naturally must to some degree call for the control of personal impulses and self-interest for the sake of something that goes beyond them. Enjoinders to control one's impulses and to sacrifice one's interests are especially appropriate to allocation issues. Hence the plausibility of the allocation criterion is further heightened by observing how it accounts nicely for the emphasis that moralities typically place upon self-control and self-sacrifice.

Morality and Complementary Relations

It is quite characteristic of several moral concepts, including the concepts of moral right and wrong, obligation, and duty, that to predicate them of the conduct of a person suggests that he stands in some sort of *reciprocal or complementary relationship with someone or something else.* Moral wrongs, for instance, are generally thought of as wrongs *against* some person, group, or institution; and a morally right action is typically (though perhaps not always) thought of as action *owed to* a person, group, or institution. Moral obligations and duties are also typically thought of as owed to someone or something. It has often been urged, in fact, that it makes no sense to speak of a moral obligation that is not an obligation *to* someone or something. Similar claims have been made about the concept of duty.

The suggestion of a complementary relationship that attaches to these concepts assumes some significance when we observe that notions of right and wrong as they are employed in *non*moral contexts do not, as a rule, convey this suggestion of complementarity. When a person draws a *wrong inference,* he has not *ipso facto* committed a wrong against any agent or agents. When we say to an artist "Putting so much orange in the background was the wrong thing to do; it has a bad effect," we are again not *ipso facto* declaring that the artist committed a wrong against anyone. There is no "injured party" in the sense in which moral wrongs tend to produce injured parties.

The feature of suggested complementarity that clings to much of our ethical discourse is, in any case, obviously quite appropriate to allocation issues. Where the right action (whatever it may be) requires an allocation of advantages among competing interests, there is an obvious sense in which right action is "owed to" the other parties to the conflict. And a wrong action, since it consists in some sort of improper allocation of advantages, will clearly produce "injured parties"; wrong actions will be wrongs *against* those whose interests deserved to be satisfied to a greater degree than they were in fact satisfied.

Is this feature of suggested complementarity another of the necessary conditions of any morality? I believe that the answer is *no*. But my reasons for rejecting complementarity as a necessary condition of morality must await the next chapter. For chapter 5 will be devoted primarily to arguments for rejecting the allocation criterion; and the feature of complementarity discussed here is so closely tied to the allocation criterion that rejection of one is tantamount to rejection of the other. The allocation criterion asserts that all moral issues are issues of possible conflict of interest; in effect, therefore, any resolution of the conflict suggests some complementarity, some trade-off of advantages. The shortcomings of a criterion in terms of complementarity are the shortcomings of the allocation criterion itself; I will defer a presentation of these shortcomings to the next chapter. The only observation I wish to urge, in concluding this section, is the observation that another property that has been widely thought to be especially characteristic of morality is nicely accounted for by the supposition that all moral issues are allocation issues.

Blame, Reproach, and Punishment

The notions of blame, reproach, and punishment are highly typical of moral evaluation. For the most part, we do not blame or reproach a person for his behavior, and do not hold him worthy of punishment, unless we think he has behaved in some *morally* objectionable way. A man is normally not blamed for an error in logical inference, nor is he thought to deserve punishment, except in special cases where his error has moral repercussions. Bad art is, likewise, not normally thought of as cause for blame; and where it *is* regarded as a cause for blame, it tends to assume the significance of a moral issue.

The prominence of these concepts in moral discourse makes good sense if we understand morality to exhibit concepts that are at home in allocation issues. All areas of evaluation may give rise to negative appraisals; but blame, reproach, and punishment represent especially severe responses to a breach of what is regarded as right. Furthermore, these concepts suggest that one is not merely pointing out where conduct has fallen short in some way, but is also *speaking for* some party or parties (perhaps only oneself) *who had a legitimate interest in the conduct.* Blame, reproach, and punishment are, in short, a kind of interference or intrusion into someone's life on the part of those who feel that what he has done is not merely his own concern, but the concern of others as well. And if we understand the offending behavior to be an action that represents an objectionable allocation of advantages in a conflict-of-interest situation, then it is not surprising that the criticism of it will be especially severe, nor is it surprising that the criticism will carry the weight of a *social* response, a response *on behalf of* persons who have an interest in how the offender has behaved.

Nevertheless, there are serious problems with use of these concepts to define the concept of morality. I will indicate briefly where the problems lie: a) The use of these concepts is not in all circumstances limited to moral issues. One may, as noted earlier, blame an infielder for dropping a pop fly ball, without thinking of his error as a moral failure. A minor breach of etiquette with no moral significance may be cause for mild reproach. And when one says "We punished the wrong man," one clearly does not imply thereby that the punished man has committed a moral offense. b) Furthermore, even where moral criticism is present, it is not clear that these concepts always apply. It is quite possible to believe that a man has behaved in a morally objectionable way, and yet neither blame nor reproach him for his failure. Certainly to regard a man as a moral offender is not *ipso facto* to favor punishment for him; there are many possible reasons for not favoring punishment for what is regarded as a moral offense, as was noted earlier. c) In any case, these concepts do not help us to identify moral *approval*. But any satisfactory analysis of the concept of morality must recognize the fact that moralities are manifested not only in negative, unfavorable reactions but in positive, favorable reactions as well.

What may we salvage from this discussion? Certainly dispositions to blame, to reproach, and to favor punishment are at least highly characteristic of moral thinking. And it is to be expected that people will tend to display such dispositions, when they are involved in conflicts of interests that require adjudication, and encounter allocations that they find objectionable. Once again, a feature that is felt to be highly characteristic of moralities is found to fit nicely into the context of allocation issues, and we have thereby found yet another reason for the plausibility of the allocation criterion.

Allocation Issues and
Generalization in Ethics

There is no need to rehearse here the prominence that discussions of generalization (in some form or other) have had in ethical theory. Philosophers have returned to the topic over and over again, and some have tried to show that a principle of generalization is by itself sufficient to provide a theory of the morally right. The topic is a notorious briar bush through which anyone must pass who would hope to provide a fully adequate theory of moral reasoning. I will not attempt to pick my way through the briar bush, but will instead skirt it cautiously, making only limited incursions into the prickly issues, and hoping merely to point out a few of the more prominent landmarks along the way. The spirit of my remarks will be that of the immediately preceding sections of this chapter: I will try to relate generalization in ethics to the allocation criterion, and will ask what it is about allocation issues that makes some form of generalization especially at home there.

What is it about allocation issues that makes generalization an appropriate response to them? Allocation issues are, it will be recalled, issues where several self-interested individuals are involved in, or threatened by, a conflict of interests, and some adjudication between these competing interests is required. Now, conflicts of interest may be "resolved" in a variety of ways, not all of which would commonly be regarded as appeals to a moral code of some kind. One or more of the parties to the conflict may bring an end to that conflict through intimidation or sheer coercion; but to take such an approach would commonly be regarded as abandoning the appeal to morality in favor of a nonmoral (or immoral) solution. If the resolution of a conflict of interest is to present even the semblance of a *moral* resolution, it must in effect be thought to have the support of reasons that could count as *general* reasons, or reasons that each party to the conflict should be able to accept as good reasons.

Disputes about moral issues typically exhibit disagreement about what sorts of reasons are general reasons, hence qualify as moral reasons, and what sorts of reasons are self-interested, private, or egocentric reasons. One man claims a benefit as his "just desert"; he says that any reasonable person, no matter what his station and position, should be able to recognize the claim as "justified" on "objective" grounds. Anyone else in a relevantly similar position would have the right to demand the same, he says. Another man disputes the claim, arguing that it has only self-interested support, not general, objective support. The first man asserts that he has *moral* reasons in support of his claim; the second denies that the reasons advanced constitute genuine moral reasons.

It would go beyond the scope of our inquiry to attempt to declare how various conflicts of interest should be resolved. To do so would be to adopt a normative stance, and to take a position regarding what are proper and good moral standards. For the purposes of this inquiry it is enough to point out that, when one is faced with an allocation issue, and attempts to achieve social harmony by resolving the conflict through use of some allocation procedures, the need naturally arises for these allocation procedures to be supported by general, objective reasons: reasons that should count as good reasons for the several parties to the conflict, and not just self-interested reasons that could have weight for only some of the parties.

To put the matter in another way: any account of some object or conduct as morally good or bad, morally right or wrong, must be thought to be made in virtue of characteristics of the object, or conduct that might reasonably be regarded by others as counting in much the same way toward its goodness or badness, rightness or wrongness.[11] If the argument of this section is sound, then such a requirement arises naturally out of a consideration of the character of allocation issues and the character of procedures needed to resolve those issues. The attempt to resolve allocation issues in the interests of social harmony naturally gives rise to the need for allocation procedures that are, in effect, thought to be supported by reasons that are "general," or "objective," or "binding on all men," or something in this vein. In brief: when morality is understood as dealing with allocation issues, the requirement for some sort of generality or universality in moral judgments makes good sense.

The above serves only as the barest outline of an approach to generalization in ethics. A great deal of technical and difficult work remains to be done, spelling out how generalization should work in moral reasoning. I will attempt here only to plug a few possible loopholes in my account, and to make it consistent with what I have said earlier.

One apparent inconsistency arises through recalling what was said in chapter 2 concerning the possibility of nonrational, "visceral" moralities. I argued there that sentiments and judgments may be identified as moral sentiments and judgments even though the person who exhibits them either does not, or can not, defend or justify himself by citing any higher rationale. To say this suggests that in order to identify opinions as moral opinions, we do not need to know the sorts of *reasons* that would be advanced in support of the opinions. In the above sketch of an approach to generalization in ethics, I seem on the other hand to be saying that an opinion may be identified as a moral opinion only if one ascertains that the reasons that are given (or would be given) in support of the opinion are thought of as reasons that would be good reasons for others as well. And this seems clearly to require that in order to identify an opinion as a moral opinion, we must know something about the reasons (justification, defense, rationale) that are or would be offered in its support. Thus, my approach to generalization in ethics seems to rule out what I have called nonrational moralities.

But it will be recalled that when speaking of nonrational moralities, I had in mind moralities that were lacking in justification *of a particular kind:* that is, justification *by way of appeal to higher normative principles.* Thus I argued that an opinion might be identifiable as a moral opinion without first ascertaining whether it was grounded in something like concern for general welfare, obedience to religious demands, or respect for custom and tradition. And I explicitly excluded from my discussion a consideration of justification in the sense of appeal to a nonethical principle such as a generalization principle. I thereby left the door open for the claim that, in order to identify an opinion as a moral opinion, it may be necessary to ascertain whether justification in this latter sense is involved.

But I would add to these qualifications some further remarks: our language has standard devices for *suggesting* generality of reasons without *explicitly claiming* generality of reasons. From the way a man speaks about an issue, we may be able to ascertain that he *in effect* believes his judgments are supportable by reasons that would be good reasons for others as well as himself, even though we do not hear him speak in terms of reasons at all. What I have in mind is the simple fact that when we *attribute a property* to something or other, we in effect suggest generality or objectivity of reasons; for if the thing does indeed have the property in question, then this is a "fact" about the thing that others who concern themselves with the thing must acknowledge also. Much of the moral talk has this character of property-attribution, thereby suggesting generality of reasons. Hence, when I judge that Jones is a man of good character or that what Jones did was highly commendable, I am attributing the properties of good character and commendability; and I thereby imply that the reasons that count as good reasons for my making these judgments are reasons that count as good reasons for others to make the same judgments.[12] The language I use is the language of objective description, the language of truth-claims about the world.

In what is said above, I do not intend to imply anything about the nature of moral "properties" and whether these properties are like or unlike properties of other kinds. My remarks are intended only to draw attention to the fact that the *language* of morality is typically the language of property-attribution, and that a judgment expressed in the language of property-attribution suggests generality or objectivity of reasons in support of the judgment.

One of the problems that I have not attempted to resolve is the problem of how one is to understand the scope of the term *others* in the requirement that moral reasons must be thought of as reasons that could count as good reasons for others, and not merely for oneself. Another problem that I have not discussed concerns proper names and egocentric terms, and how they may figure in moral judgments, principles, reasons, and the like—if at all. For the moment I wish to claim only the following: a) A morality must serve to evaluate and direct conduct; and the evaluations and prescriptions that it issues are characteristically thought of as objective claims; that is, they are *in effect* thought to be such that the reasons in their support could count as good reasons not only for the person who issues them, but for others as well. And b) this characteristic of objectivity or generality of reasons that moralities exhibit makes especially good sense in response to allocation issues, and thus further contributes to the plausibility of the allocation criterion.

Review and Conclusion

Let us take stock. If we accept the allocation criterion as a necessary mark of the moral, and hold that all moral issues are allocation issues, then we are provided with a convenient explanation for a number of common beliefs and claims about morality. The beliefs and claims that are thereby accounted for are the following:

1. Moral issues are frequently and typically thought to be such that the group or larger community has a significant stake in how they are resolved. Whether or not an individual follows a moral principle is typically thought to be not merely "up to him" or "his own business" but "of legitimate concern to others." Moral issues

are typically thought to be issues that are of "special social importance." These features are all stated in admittedly quite imprecise terms. In my discussion of them I suggested that, a) they are best interpreted as entailing the propriety of *social interference,* or *social sanctions,* as a means of regulating the resolution of an issue; b) such a feature (that social sanctions are favored) is not *essential* to moral issues, despite the claims of some philosophers and anthropologists, since one can regard an issue as a moral issue without favoring social sanctions as a means of dealing with it; but, c) the supposition that moral issues are allocation issues nevertheless helps to explain why social sanctions and group involvement in the resolution of an issue have been *widely associated* with morality.

2. Another characteristic of morality that is neatly accounted for by the allocation criterion is the relatively great emphasis that moralities place upon self-control, self-restraint, and self-sacrifice. Where a conflict of interest is at stake, any resolution of the conflict naturally calls for at least some parties to the conflict to forgo their self-interest.

3. The allocation criterion also readily explains the suggestion of reciprocity or complementarity that attaches to many moral predicates (e.g., morally wrong action as a wrong committed *against* someone, morally right action as action *owed to* someone).

4. Blame, reproach, and punishment are especially characteristic responses to failures that are regarded as *moral* transgressions. They constitute relatively severe reactions to violation of a norm or standard; and the prominence of severe responses of this sort in morality is quite understandable if we take moral issues to be allocation issues. For in allocation issues, a wrongful step

produces injured parties, who may be expected to react strongly since their interests have been frustrated.

5. The allocation criterion makes good sense of the fact that judgments about resolution of a moral issue are typically thought to be supported by general, interpersonal reasons—reasons that are thought to count as valid reasons not only for oneself but for others as well.

In closing, I may add a few further observations about why the allocation criterion may seem attractive. Consider first the Golden Rule, which many people regard as the paradigm of a moral principle. "Do unto others as you would have them do unto you" might readily be rendered in the following manner: "Satisfy the interests of others as you would like them to satisfy your own interests." Such a formulation clearly suggests a context in which interests are at stake and where some trade-off of interest-satisfaction is called for; in short, it is a formulation that seems to have appropriate application in allocation issues. Consider, second, a characteristic form of moral rebuke and how it contrasts with nonmoral criticism. The form of rebuke I have in mind is "You had no right to do that." Now, criticisms of a *non*moral kind—say, in aesthetics, or etiquette, or prudential matters, or logic—may naturally be expressed by the utterance "That was the wrong thing to do." But the judgment "You had no right to do that" sounds less appropriate in these areas, and is much more suggestive of a moral objection. If moral issues are understood as allocation issues, then the "You have no right" locution is readily interpreted: it becomes a way of saying not merely that a wrong action was committed, but also a way of suggesting that the wrong action impinged upon the legitimate interests of some other party. It becomes, in other words, a way of saying that a conflict of interests was improperly resolved. Consider, finally, the naturalness of the claims that learning to live a moral life is a matter of learning how to "get along with others," learning to "look out for the other guy," learning to sacrifice one's interests when the interests of others are at stake, and so on. All of these expressions suggest that moral principles are essentially principles having to do with how conflicting interests are to be dealt with in a reasonable manner.

It seems clear that if any genuine social group is to survive, the group must adhere to some principles and procedures for resolving conflicts of interest, so that a degree of social harmony is preserved. What is more natural than to claim that the definitive mark of moralities is that they are intended to fill this need? And when this understanding of morality helps to explain the widespread feeling of special social involvement in moral issues; when it accounts for the special emphasis that morality places upon self-control and self-sacrifice; when it accounts for the reciprocity suggested by many moral judgments; when it explains the prominence of blame, reproach, and punishment in moral behavior; and when it gives an account of why genuine moral reasons are felt to be interpersonal and general—then such an understanding of morality would seem to have a very strong claim to be accepted as the only correct one.

1. R. B. Perry, *Realms of Value,* quoted in *Problems of Moral Philosophy,* ed. Paul Taylor (Belmont, Calif.: Dickenson Publishing Co., Inc., 1967), p. 20.
2. Stephen Toulmin, *The Place of Reason in Ethics* (Cambridge: Cambridge University Press, 1950), p. 145.
3. Kurt Baier, *The Moral Point of View,* abridged ed. (New York: Random House, 1965), p. 96.
4. W. K. Frankena, "Recent Conceptions of Morality," *Morality and the Language of Conduct,* ed. Castaneda and Nakhnikian (Detroit, Mich.: Wayne State University Press, 1963), p. 9. Although in this passage Frankena is merely de-

scribing the position and not espousing it, later in the same article he explicitly defends the position.

5. For the sake of simplifying discussion, I shall not concern myself with the possibility of a morality that takes as its objects of concern *solely* nonhuman beings. (A misanthropic animal-lover might possibly have such a morality; the scope of his moral concern would extend solely to animals.)

6. My discussion here may perhaps seem to blur the distinction between morality and *law*. For use of terms such as *prescription, directive,* and especially *code of behavior* may suggest that I am speaking of a body of promulgated regulations and/or laws, perhaps recorded or laid down in some way. What I have in mind is, however, morality in the sense of a body of action-guiding beliefs, attitudes, and dispositions that naturally issue in value-judgments about what has been done and what should be done. (See chapter 1, opening paragraph.) There is a natural sense in which such action-guiding beliefs, attitudes, and dispositions may be said to constitute a personal "code of behavior" (or a shared "code of behavior") that is quite distinct from promulgated law.

7. After hitting independently upon these locutions, I found that they are used for a somewhat similar purpose by Kurt Baier, in his article "Moral Obligation," *Amiercan Philosophical Quarterly* 3, no. 3 (July, 1966). See especially pp. 223-26. I am indebted to this article for helping me to clarify and expand my own position. But I disagree with Baier in that he takes a criterion that is rather like my "allocation criterion" as a necessary condition of any morality.

8. A. MacBeath, *Experiments in Living* (New York: Macmillan, 1952), p. 150.

9. See chapter 2, n32.

10. Pp. 224f.

11. When I say "might reasonably be regarded by others as counting in much the same way . . ." I mean not "would be *effective in causing* others to take the same attitude," but "could properly count as valid reasons for others to take the same attitude." Pointing out a characteristic of some object or conduct to another person (e.g., that it is ugly) may cause another to share a moral attitude toward it, without constituting a valid reason for adopting that attitude.

12. Reasons for making a judgment are not, of course, necessarily identical with reasons for expressing a judgment in an actual speech act. I may have good reasons for making a given judgment about Jones, yet also good reasons for keeping my mouth shut and not giving voice to my judgment. The good reasons I speak of in this passage are to be understood as good reasons for making a judgment, not as good reasons for giving utterance to a judgment.

5
Utility and Social Harmony: II

> The concept of morality itself bears the accumulated
> scars of conceptual evolution. Its multiple associations are a
> bar to summing it up in any one way.[1]
>
> —W. D. Falk

According to the allocation criterion, a morality necessarily places some value on satisfaction of interest and
social harmony; according to the allocation criterion, no
system of action-guiding value-beliefs and attitudes can
count as a morality unless those who adhere to it prescribe and evaluate conduct as right or wrong at least
partly on grounds of the allocation of advantages and
consequent satisfaction of interest that they expect the
conduct to produce. In chapter 4, the allocation criterion fared well. It was found to be attractive and plausible on numerous grounds, and we examined several
possible reasons for the fact that some moral
philosophers have apparently believed it—or something
like it—to be a necessary mark of the moral. In this
chapter the allocation criterion will, however, come
under fire; the chapter will present a variety of arguments intended to show that the allocation criterion is
not a necessary condition of a moral code.

Before the task of refutation of the allocation criterion
is undertaken, however, that criterion must be made
more precise. In our discussion in chapter 4 of the
plausibility of the criterion, it was enough for our purposes to discuss a fairly loosely formulated version. But

when we turn to refutation of the criterion, some additional distinctions and qualifications are called for. As it turns out, there are several different but related criteria, each of which might reasonably be called an allocation criterion, and each of which might be advanced as a necessary condition of any morality. The objections to any one of these criteria will not necessarily hold against all other versions. Thus, before I attempt to refute "the" allocation criterion, I will introduce some distinctions and refinements that hopefully will clarify the criteria to be discussed.

In considering various versions of the allocation criterion, perhaps the most fundamental distinction to be drawn is between criteria that require of any morality that its adherents *appeal* in some *explicit* way to allocational considerations when they justify their moral sentiments, and criteria that require of any morality that it *in fact* serve an allocational function, whether or not the adherents of the morality explicitly appeal to allocational considerations in their beliefs about the morality. This distinction may be termed the distinction between *criteria of explicit appeal* and *criteria of objective role*. According to the former group of criteria, what matters in identifying a morality are the beliefs concerning allocation held by those who adhere to the morality; according to the latter group of criteria, what matters in identifying a morality is the actual role the morality plays or has played in the behavior of individuals and groups. According to one version of the former, belief about a certain practice might count as a moral belief because the person holding the belief also believes that the practice will promote social harmony. According to one version of the latter, belief about a certain practice might count as a moral belief because the belief in fact serves a sociological function of promoting social harmony, whether the person realizes this fact or not.

In the following discussion I will first consider criteria of explicit appeal and second, criteria of objective role. I will examine the following possible variations of an allocation criterion.[2]

A) Criteria of explicit appeal:
1) Teleological versus deontological criteria.
2) Criteria concerning basic moral principles versus criteria concerning subsidiary moral principles.
3) Criteria that require that the basic normative principles be allocational versus criteria that require that the epistemic justification of these moral principles be allocational.
4) Criteria that require that any morality be purely allocational versus criteria that require only that any morality be partly allocational.
B) Criteria of objective role:
1) Psychological criteria: criteria concerning covert, subconscious beliefs regarding allocation issues.
2) Functional (sociological) criteria: criteria concerning the actual function of moralities and moral beliefs in the resolution of allocation issues.
3) Evolutionary criteria: criteria concerning the sociological-historical origin of moralities out of allocation issues.

Criteria of Explicit Appeal

Among criteria of explicit appeal, the first distinction to be considered is that between teleological criteria and deontological criteria. A teleological allocation criterion might be formulated as follows: any system of action-guiding beliefs and attitudes that is to count as a morality must be intended to deal with allocation of advantages among persons with competing interests, and must evaluate solely on the basis of *maximization of satisfaction* among the competing parties. A deontological allocation criterion might, on the other hand, be formulated as follows: any system of action-guiding beliefs and attitudes that is to count as a morality must be intended to deal with allocation of advantages among persons with competing interests, and must evaluate at least partly on the basis of the *sheer form of the allocation,* apart from the question of the degree to which satisfaction is maximized.

Now, I think it can be readily seen that each of these formulations is too restrictive. The first criterion rules out formalistic moralities such as that of W. D. Ross; the second criterion rules out standard act-utilitarianism. In its most plausible form, the allocation criterion admits *both* teleological and deontological moralities. Furthermore, most of the arguments I will offer against the allocation criterion are arguments that tell equally against teleological and deontological versions of the criterion. It is desirable, therefore, to formulate the allocation criterion so that it is *neutral* with respect to these alternatives. I offer the following as such a formulation: any system of action-guiding beliefs and attitudes that is to count as a morality must adjudicate between persons with competing interests according to *some* conception of what is a desirable or proper allocation of advantages. Such a formulation admits both ordinary utilitarianism and formalistic accounts of morality such as that of Ross; but it excludes codes of behavior that do not in any way evaluate in terms of what is considered to be a desirable or proper allocation of advantages among interpersonal conflicts of interest. Thus, according to this formulation, every morality must place some value upon some sort of interpersonal conflict resolution, regardless of whether that resolution is to be effected by teleological or deontological principles.

The mention of principles introduces the second distinction to be considered among criteria of explicit appeal. An allocation criterion might require that allocational considerations enter into a morality at a basic level of moral principles; it might require that allocational considerations occur at every level of moral evaluation; or it might require that allocational considerations enter in only at some level or other of moral evaluation. Now, it is surely implausible to insist that at every level of moral evaluation, moral principles must be explicitly allocational. Most of us would recognize a moral imperative not to drive at excessive speeds on public highways; yet such an imperative is not *per se* allocational. We recognize its allocational significance when we consider that driving at excessive speeds is dangerous to others on the road, and thereby comes under some more general principle such as "Do not indulge minor whims if doing so significantly imperils the well-being of others." It is not the case that moral principles of every level must be explicitly allocational.

Furthermore, it would seem that in order to meet a plausible version of the allocation criterion, moral evaluation must be more than *incidentally* or *accidentally* allocational. The point of a significant allocation criterion must be to require that moralities evaluate *on the basis of* allocational considerations. A principle may happen to provide for allocation of advantages without evaluating on the basis of that allocation; such a principle should not, I think, count as meeting a significant version of the allocation criterion. For instance, it may be a fairly reliable maxim that employers who wish to get good work out of their employees should pay the employees well; but the principle "To achieve a better product, pay your employees well" should not count as a principle that meets the allocation criterion. Despite the fact that the principle provides for allocation of advantages, it places no basic value as such on that allocation; it merely happens to be the case that an allocation of advantages is an appropriate means to a nonallocational end. The version of the allocation criterion that deserves to be considered is one that declares that it is intrinsic to every morality that it place some value upon how advantages are allocated in a conflict-of-interest situation. The point of the criterion is that it is precisely the fact that the basic values of the value-system are allocational that helps to identify it as a morality. Subsidiary moral principles may not be allocational; but the basic moral principles upon which they rest must be directed to the allocation of advantages.

Thus, I propose the following refinement of the allocation criterion: any system of action-guiding beliefs and attitudes that is to count as a morality must adjudicate between persons with competing interests according to some conception of what is a desirable or proper allocation of advantages, and the basic principles or premises of the system must themselves be principles of adjudication or allocation of advantages.

But this formulation raises some new questions and calls for yet another refinement. When one speaks of the "basic principles or premises" of a value system, one may be speaking of more than one sort of thing. A system of value typically has some substantive principles that are more fundamental than others, and probably includes some values that may be called "basic" or "ultimate." But these basic or ultimate value principles may themselves be supported by what philosophers would call an epistemology: some sort of argument structure that provides justification or support for the adoption of the basic or ultimate values. In the writings of many moral philosophers, the distinction is apparent. Thus the ultimate, substantive value principles of Ross's moral theory are his list of *prima facie* duties; but he supports the selection of these principles by the contention that they are synthetic *a priori* truths, knowable by careful intellectual intuition. Mill's principle that happiness and only happiness is intrinsically desirable is supported by arguments which themselves are not substantive normative assertions, but rather considerations that are intended to show that the only psychologically plausible position is that which asserts that happiness is the supreme good. And so on.

Thus, one must distinguish between the basic, substantive value premises or principles of a moral system and the epistemic arguments (if any) that are offered as justification for accepting the value premises or principles as the correct ones. We may ask, then, to which of these kinds of "basic principle" the allocation criterion is intended to apply. Is the epistemic foundation of a moral system to be allocational? are the basic value principles to be allocational? or both?

Among those who advocate some version of the allocation criterion, I do not believe that this distinction has always been clearly made. But I believe that the spirit of the various proposals is fairly obvious. It is not the *arguments for* a set of basic moral principles that are to meet the allocation criterion; it is those basic moral principles themselves to which the allocation criterion applies. For instance, Ross's discussion of intellectual intuition does not appeal to allocational considerations, but his list of *prima facie* duties clearly includes some allocation principles; and it is by virtue of this latter fact that his moral theory meets the allocation criterion. And when Perry declares that "Morality is man's endeavor to harmonize conflicting interests . . . ," he is clearly speaking of the fundamental, substantive value principles of morality, not the epistemology that might be offered in support of those principles.

Hence, yet another qualification of the allocation criterion is called for. We must now formulate the criterion as follows: any system of action-guiding beliefs and attitudes that is to count as a morality must adjudicate between persons with competing interests according to some conception of what is a desirable or proper allocation of advantages, and the basic *normative* principles or *value* premises of the system must themselves be principles of adjudication or allocation of advantages.

There remains one other variation among criteria of explicit appeal that we must consider. It might be maintained that anything that is to count as a morality must be *purely* allocational in the sense that *every* moral judgment must ultimately rest in an allocation principle of some kind; or it might instead be maintained only that at least *some* judgments of any moral system must ultimately rest in allocation principles. Put differently, it might be maintained that all of the basic normative principles of a moral system must be allocational or, instead, only that some must be. The former may be called a strong allocation principle, the latter a weak allocation principle. A morality that met the weaker criterion but not the stronger would be partly allocational, partly not.

Since the weaker version claims less, it will be more difficult to refute. For in order to refute it, we must show not only that a morality may be partly nonallocational, but that it may be wholly nonallocational. Nevertheless, I shall undertake to refute the weaker version; I shall undertake, that is, to show that moralities may exist that to no degree are based on principles that are allocational. Refutation of the weaker version will, of course, constitute refutation of the stronger version also. The version of the allocation principle that I shall attempt to refute is, then, the following: any system of action-guiding beliefs and attitudes that is to count as a morality must adjudicate between persons with competing interests according to some conception of what is a desirable or proper allocation of advantages, and *at least some* of the basic normative principles or value premises of the system must themselves be principles of adjudication or allocation of advantages.

For our purposes, the above may be taken as the definitive version of an allocation principle of explicit appeal. But since it is somewhat redundant, I will for the sake of convenience put the criterion in the following, abbreviated form: any system of action-guiding beliefs and attitudes that is to count as a morality must be such that at least some of the basic normative principles of the system are principles of allocation of advantages among persons with competing interests. Or, more briefly yet: every morality must in part appeal to basic principles intended to resolve interpersonal conflicts of interest. To resolve social conflict is to promote nonconflict; and to promote nonconflict is, loosely speaking, to promote social harmony. Hence we may say that the allocation criterion requires of every morality that it place some basic value on social harmony.

Shortcomings of the Allocation Criterion of Explicit Appeal

What are the objections to the allocation criterion, as formulated above? In the pages that immediately follow, I offer a number of reasons for rejecting the criterion. The first six of these objections are of a rather general nature, and I do not regard them as entirely decisive by themselves. Objections 7 through 11, on the other hand, purport to offer rather more compelling grounds for denying that the allocation criterion states a necessary mark of every morality.

We may begin by reminding ourselves that the allocation criterion seeks to separate the moral from the nonmoral by defining moralities in terms of appeal to a particular kind of higher normative principle. To insist upon the allocation criterion is to say that no system of value can count as a morality unless its evaluations and prescriptions concerning conduct are to be justified, or backed up, at least partly in terms of the way the conduct is believed to resolve conflict and promote social harmony. It is to say that every person who has a morality must appeal in part to satisfaction of interest and social harmony in making and defending his moral judgments. But such a requirement seems objectionable for the following reasons:

1. Many systems of value do not make ultimate appeal to satisfaction of interest and social harmony, yet otherwise display what may be called the "typical machinery

of a morality." That is, they a) govern personal and group behavior, b) issue judgments of praise and blame, c) employ notions ,f honor and integrity, d) evaluate dispositions and personal traits, e) give rise to social sanctions, and to such feelings as guilt and remorse when the values are violated, and f) seek to control present impulses for the sake of long-range and interpersonal goals. The presence of such characteristics seems to me to argue strongly in favor of treating these systems of value as moralities.

This line of criticism is admittedly not conclusive by itself; it is merely programmatic and incomplete. For it to be decisive, we would have to establish that the characteristics cited above are *sufficient* to constitute a code of behavior as a morality, a task not attempted in this study. Nevertheless, the fact that a code of behavior may exhibit all of the cited characteristics, which are typical of moral codes, without meeting the allocation criterion, is a fact that should, I believe, create at least some doubt that the allocation criterion is necessary.

2. A survey of moralities and putative moralities from different cultures and different eras suggests that the character of the higher normative principles used to defend a system of value governing social behavior is as much a function of the prevailing scientific, metaphysical, and religious views as it is an expression of the essential features of the functioning value-system itself. What is given as the rationale for a value-system is, in other words, strongly influenced by the current body of factual beliefs, and to an outsider may readily appear as rationalization, or as a kind of "stage-setting," for the moral system. In our own culture we often hear people defend their moral views in outlandish and irrelevant ways. Again, recognition of opinions as moral opinions

does not seem to be particularly contingent upon ascertaining the kinds of higher principles that a person uses to defend the opinions.

3. A restriction such as the allocation criterion appears to run counter to established usage in the social and behavioral sciences. Almost from its inception as a discipline, social anthropology has included within the category of *morality*, or *morals*, codes that the allocation criterion would exclude. Psychological studies of "moral" development do not generally limit themselves in this way, either; Kohlberg's cross-cultural comparison of moral development is only one example.[3] The great latitude of the concept of morality as generally acknowledged by social scientists is aptly illustrated by two major volumes concerning different moral systems: L. T. Hobhouse's *Morals in Evolution*[4] and Vergilius Ferm's *Encyclopedia of Morals*.[5]

4. Perhaps under the influence of the above-mentioned disciplines, I believe that good ordinary usage now generally countenances a conception of morality according to which it is correct to speak of the "moralities" of other persons or cultures, even where those moralities are apparently not grounded in terms of satisfaction of interest and social harmony.

5. Perhaps a more compelling reason than those given in 3 and 4 is the fact that codes of behavior that lack characteristics required by the allocation criterion may have very significant *structural and functional* similarities to those which meet the criterion. (One is reminded here of the "typical machinery of morality," cited in the first objection.) These structural analogies and similarities are presumably the chief reason that social and behavioral scientists use the term in the broad way they do.

6. As a further consideration, it may be added that the theoretic richness and usefulness of a concept is enhanced when it is understood as applying to phenomena that are in important, significant ways similar to each other. It is possible to cling to a restricted notion of morality that would make the term applicable only to those codes whose basic principles are intended to promote social harmony. But if we are to understand better the role that such codes play in the lives of the individuals and groups who adhere to them, it will probably be enlightening to understand them as part of a larger family of value-systems that they functionally resemble. The similarities may prove more enlightening than the differences, making reasonable the application of the term *morality* to all members of the family.

In chapter 3 I noted that the term *morality* has no one, fixed meaning in ordinary language, and that any attempt at philosophical analysis requires something like a linguistic decision to focus upon a portion of the total variety of contexts in which the term is more or less correctly used. I have, in effect, opted for a broad conception of morality, and have cited the above reasons as partial justification. But readers who continue to believe that a morality must be more narrowly defined are likely to see my rejection of the position discussed in this chapter as thereby simply rendered true by linguistic fiat. The result, they may feel, is to quiet dissenters without resolving any real questions of principle. And the questions of principle here are of considerable importance. The conception of morality as intrinsically concerned with social welfare and harmony has exercised a powerful hold over Western moral philosophy. For Plato, the concepts of a moral man and society were closely tied to concepts of harmony in the individual and in the state;

and for perhaps most of the major moral philosophers of the Western tradition, including Hobbes, Locke, Hume, and Mill, morality was seen as connected in some intimate way with the governance of social interaction for purposes of satisfaction of human interests. In view of the strength of this tradition and the plausibility of many of its presuppositions, some further discussion is probably called for before I may safely reject the claim that moralities necessarily have as their intended purpose the resolution of conflict and the satisfaction of interest.

I offer these further lines of objection to the allocation criterion:

7. Suppose we set aside the case of pure egoism, and for the moment disregard also the possibility of duties to oneself, in the sense in which one may think of oneself as (in effect) two persons, one owing moral responsibility to the other. (In this vein, one might say to oneself "I owe it to my future self not to imperil my health in later years by smoking cigarettes now.") Then, according to the position being discussed and criticized, a man could not *without logically contradicting himself* believe both that a) he was the only being in existence; no other beings existed who could possible have satisfiable interests; and b) he was morally responsible in some way or other. Yet this seems to be an unacceptable conclusion. If I were this last person alive, I would probably not regard myself as subject to any moral rules, and perhaps the reader agrees with me. But this is beside the point. We are concerned not with what we regard as reasonable moralities, but with all logically possible moralities. And it seems logically possible for a last person alive to adhere to a morality, however odd or eccentric or irrational it might seem to us. Perhaps this person simply

feels obligated to bathe every day. Perhaps he accepts certain sexual prohibitions as applying to himself. Or perhaps he adheres to an impersonal sort of religion that entails no assumptions about the existence of divine beings with satisfiable interests, but nevertheless gives rise to rules of conduct that he thinks of in moral terms. A last person alive might, if he violated his code of conduct, feel guilty; he might feel that he was an appropriate object of moral condemnation, and could legitimately be morally condemned, were anyone else alive to express that condemnation. He might, in short, sincerely believe that he had behaved in a morally objectionable fashion without at the same time believing that his behavior might conceivably have consequences for the satisfaction of interest and social harmony. It would seem to follow that the concept of morality is not analytically connected with considerations of consequences of this type.

8. The possibility of nonrational, "visceral" moralities seems to argue against the position we are discussing. For if a man may have recognizably moral sentiments without being able to defend those sentiments in terms of higher normative principles, let alone in terms of interest-satisfaction and social harmony, then the claim would seem to be false that codes of conduct are identifiable as moralities only if they appeal to ends of interest-satisfaction and social harmony.

9. Despite the fact that it admits many (perhaps most) deontological theories, the allocation criterion rules out by definition at least some purely formalistic accounts of morality. If it is true, then any code of conduct that declares behavior to be right or wrong not in terms of allocation but solely in terms of some other purely formalistic criterion, such as logical universalizability, could not

count as a morality. It has the consequence that when a person says "I just believe it's morally wrong to do x, quite independently of the significance of x for allocation of advantages and social harmony," that person is talking nonsense. According to the allocation criterion, the belief this person professes to hold is not merely mistaken but logically incoherent.

Now it may well be that no purely formalistic system of this kind can satisfy the requirements for an acceptable normative moral theory. Whether this is the case is not, however, the issue before us. The issue is not whether such a code could be an acceptable moral code, but whether it could be a moral code at all. And to declare that any nonallocational formalistic code is, by the definition of morality, not a morality at all, seems to impose an unreasonably arbitrary restriction upon the concept of morality.

10. The position that morality necessarily appeals to satisfaction of interest and social harmony as justifying values appears to slight the major role that religious justification has played in the defense of moral principles, both in Western society and elsewhere. The Edels remark that "it is clear from even the most limited kind of survey [of various moralities] that there are at least three different basic avenues of justification which occur quite commonly. We may call them custom, religion, and human well-being."[6] Emile Durkheim, in his critique of the British utilitarians, denies that moralities always appeal to human well-being; Kohlberg summarizes Durkheim as follows: "While modern Western societies divorce morality from religion, the basic moral rules and attitudes in many groups are those concerning relations to gods, not men, and hence do not center on human-welfare consequences."[7] But religious appeals as a basis

for moral principles have been very prevalent in Western societies, also. Ivan Karamazov's cry "If God is dead, then anything is permitted!" could hardly have the force it does for many Western persons, were this not the case.

It might be argued that although the appeal to religion frequently figures heavily in justification of moral principles, always somehow back of that religious appeal is the thought, implicit or explicit, that human welfare and social harmony are at stake; that we are to adhere to the demands of religion only because such adherence makes for the welfare of us all. God knows best for us, it may be said, and He has our own interests at heart; thus we should obey Him. Now there is no doubt that this is a very common theme in religious justification of moral principles; but that it is the *only* such theme is not so clear. Is it not possible, and indeed fairly common, for a man to believe that his moral duties rest on religious demands, quite apart from whether adherence to religious demands makes for human well-being and social harmony? "Who are we, to assume that God concerns himself with what will benefit us? We are his creatures, and must obey Him; that is all we need to know," such a man might say. The Edels aptly characterize such a viewpoint:

> In general, the basic principle underlying the whole code is the picture of God as authoritative source and model of what is right. The stopping-point on which the whole moral edifice rests is the principle that it is the role and whole duty of man to obey God. This together with the picture of God and His relation to man, is the justificatory essence; the threats of punishment are not the meaning of evil but extra, supportive sanctions.[8]

Yet the contention that God's will constitutes the ultimate appeal in morality contains an ambiguity. It is an ambiguity that was examined earlier in this chapter: the ambiguity between the basic normative principles of a moral scheme and the ultimate epistemic justification for those principles. A person who wished to defend the allocation criterion while recognizing the possibility of a theistic foundation for morality might argue as follows: "Granted, a morality may be grounded in a conception of God as the ultimate moral authority. But to adhere to such a theistically grounded morality is simply to regard God as the source of moral knowledge. Knowledge of God's will then becomes the epistemic foundation for the basic principles of morality. But in order for these principles to count as moral principles, they must still be allocational. In order for God to be promulgating a morality, rather than some nonmoral code, he must promulgate principles that meet the allocation criterion."

This objection has considerable force; but I think it overlooks some possible versions of a theistically grounded morality. In particular, it overlooks the possibility of a "voluntaristic" outlook, according to which God's will is not the clue to what is right and wrong, but is *definitive* of right and wrong. According to such an account, the principle "Whatever God wills is right" is not an observation that God is morally omniscient (and benevolent); it is, rather, a substantive normative principle to the effect that God's willing of some form of conduct *makes* that conduct right. The principle thus is not the epistemic foundation for the substantive normative principles; it is itself *the* substantive normative principle of the morality. And it is nonallocational. Thus I think the allocation criterion fails to encompass at least one dimension of religiously based morality.

One can imagine a hypothetical medieval philosopher

arguing that the sole basis for any possible morality lies in the sheer requirements of religion, and that the notion of human well-being and social harmony is logically extraneous to morality. To assume that the chief point of moralities in the divine plan is to promote satisfaction of interest and social harmony is an example of *hubris,* he might argue.

11. Somewhat similar remarks might be made for the appeal to custom in defense of moral principles. "That's just the way it's always done" or "That's just the custom of the group" may appear to be poor defenses of a moral judgment to most of us; but for many persons, they are felt to be quite sufficient in themselves, and seem to be proffered without any particular thought of interest-satisfaction or allocation of advantages in conflict-of-interest situations. To quote Kohlberg again on Durkheim: "The mere fact of the existence of an institutionalized rule endows it with moral sacredness, regardless of its human-welfare consequences."[9] Kohlberg regards this sheer appeal to custom and the authority of the group as characteristic of the earlier stages of moral development, with an appeal to human-welfare consequences being made only at later stages.[10]

To a person who argued that custom-based moralities simply exhibit the belief that custom is a reliable moral authority, and that the moral principles enthroned in custom must still be allocational, I would make a reply similar to that made in the previous section: in some cases, custom appears to be regarded not merely as the epistemic authority in morality but as definitive of morality. To repeat Durkheim's view: "The mere fact of the existence of an institutionalized rule endows it with moral sacredness. . . ."

I conclude, on the basis of the foregoing discussion,

that it is not a necessary condition of any morality that it place some value on interest satisfaction and social harmony. There are conceivable and even actual moralities that do not evaluate in these terms and are not defended in these terms. The allocation criterion of explicit appeal does not state a necessary condition for anything that could count as a morality.

Two Counterexamples

My arguments in this chapter have been presented largely as appeals to the reader's considered reflection and linguistic intuition about proper usage of the words *moral* and *morality*. The arguments leave much to the rational discretion of the reader. Are there other modes of argument available to us that might be effectively employed in refutation of the allocation criterion, in the absence of a complete account of the marks of the moral? I do not see what these further modes of argument might be. But I think the type of argument already used might perhaps be employed in a particular way that will help to reinforce and solidify the refutation of the allocation criterion. What I have in mind is the presentation of a couple of putative counterexamples to the allocation criterion, described in fuller detail than any heretofore presented. Although these cannot be proffered as absolutely "hard" counterexamples (counterexamples absolutely impervious to rebuttal), they may perhaps come fairly close to being decisive. In describing them I will not offer any radically new considerations, but will draw largely upon arguments already presented in chapters 4 and 5. Nevertheless, the counterexamples may serve as a focal point around which previous arguments may be centered, in such a way as to give greater force to those arguments.

Case 1: Jacoby, the Sexual Conservative

Imagine a man named Jacoby, who is a conservative regarding sexual morality. Jacoby has strong objections to certain kinds of unusual sexual practices; he regards these practices as "dirty, disgusting, and immoral." Jacoby is unmoved by the observation that such practices do not hurt anyone, and may even be fun. That's irrelevant, he says; such practices are simply wrong, and that's that. People "don't have the right" to engage in the practices, he says; whether one engages in the practices is not just his own business. Jacoby admits that these practices may involve no significant conflicts of interest, so that engaging in them will not hurt anyone, and upon inquiry it becomes clear that his objections are not based on the particular allocation of satisfaction that is involved in the practices. There is nothing wrong or unfair about the allocation of satisfaction *per se,* he thinks. It is the sheer form of the practices that is objectionable to him; and the practices would be objectionable on the same grounds even if they in fact had no particular significance for allocation of advantages and interest-satisfaction.

Notice that Jacoby does not think of the sexual practices as *wrongs against* any persons or groups; his objections are directed against the form of the practices, and are not based upon how the practices parcel out pains or pleasures. He admits, in fact, that there are no "injured parties" as a consequence of the practices.

We may further suppose Jacoby to favor the enactment (or retaining) of laws providing severe penalties for persons caught engaging in the practices. We may suppose him to regard with great favor anyone who is instrumental in discouraging the practices. Perhaps Jacoby was once tempted to engage in the practices himself, and the mere fact of feeling such temptation was so troubling to him that he achieved relief from his self-castigation only by going to his confessor (or psychiatrist) and relating his feelings.

If the reader is somewhat troubled by the apparent absence of any appeal by Jacoby to more general normative principles as a means of justification for his objections to the practices, then we may alter the picture slightly by allowing Jacoby to appeal to "higher" principles, which nevertheless have nothing to do with conflict-resolution and satisfaction of interest. The practices are wrong, says Jacoby, simply because God prohibits them and we should obey God's will. Or the practices, despite the fact that their consequences are harmless, are "contrary to nature" and "abnormal."

Jacoby believes that the injunction against the practices applies to all men, regardless of the society in which they live. For a society in which such practices were permitted, Jacoby would have harsh condemnation. At best, members of such a society are deserving of pity, and stand in need of cleansing reform by moral missionaries who are more "enlightened" and "morally sophisticated."

Can we seriously deny that Jacoby has *moral* objections to the practices, and regards it as a significant *moral* issue whether a person or group engages in them? Yet, if my description has been successful, the picture we have of Jacoby is that of a man with no concern for allocation issues, at least so far as his sexual conservatism is concerned. Jacoby has recognizably moral views that do not meet the allocation criterion. Furthermore, we may imagine Jacoby to have other similar moral views that together may readily be called a morality.

Case 2: McNab, the Stoic

McNab is a devotee of the writings of Epictetus and Marcus Aurelius. His first encounter with stoic thought filled him with a sense of revelation, intellectual excitement, and spiritual discovery; and he is now thoroughly captivated by the ideal of a life lived in accordance with stoic precepts. What attracts him to stoicism is not so much that side of stoicism which calls for devoted public service; the attractiveness of stoicism for McNab lies in the recipe it seems to provide for a personally satisfying and edifying life. McNab seeks, above all, a *mastery of himself:* control over his emotions, patience with matters beyond his control, and a self-discipline that enables him to face disruptive elements with equanimity. He believes firmly that the universe is rationally ordered; apparent flaws in the scheme of things are really illusory. Hence frustrations, problems, and conflicts have little effect upon McNab; they belong to the surface of life, not its substance, and McNab has achieved a psychic distance from them that enables him to maintain an inner peace of mind. McNab is caught up in the pursuit of a *personal summum bonum;* he governs his thoughts and behavior according to principles whose purpose is to provide for a rewarding, personally satisfying life style.

McNab is, however, a pluralist with regard to the question of what style of life is most desirable and satisfactory. Although he has found his own spiritual home in stoicism, he believes that stoicism does not provide a universally viable way of life; he recognizes that other persons, with other temperaments, might find it to be stultifying and would do well to seek out other life-styles instead. Certainly McNab does not believe that stoic precepts should be imposed on others, nor is he even particularly motivated to urge others to adopt them.

Furthermore, McNab is not committed to stoicism because he sees it as the answer to conflicts within the social order. Although it might well be the case that if everyone were a thoroughgoing stoic, major social conflicts would not arise, McNab would see this as only an incidental, although fortunate, by-product of stoicism. McNab does not value stoicism for the resolutions (if any) that it offers for issues involving social conflicts of interest; he values it for the quality of life it makes possible for him personally.

I think we must say that McNab's commitment to stoicism constitutes commitment to a *morality*. If one were to ask what McNab's moral convictions are, the proper response would surely be to cite the stoic precepts that guide his thought and behavior. I think it is also the case that McNab's morality does not meet the allocation criterion. For the chief point of the stoic code, in the form in which McNab adheres to it, is not to allocate advantages in conflict-of-interest situations; allocation of advantages among competing individuals is merely incidental to living McNab's version of the stoic life.

It might be objected that although McNab's stoicism does not concern itself significantly with resolution of conflict among persons, it *does* concern itself with satisfaction of interests—McNab's personal interests. Furthermore, it seeks to *harmonize* those interests, for the sake of McNab's "peace of mind." A basic value in stoicism is, indeed, inner harmony and equanimity. Hence it might be argued that McNab's stoicism does meet the allocation criterion after all.

In reply to this objection, I might argue that the allocation criterion, as discussed in the many pages above, placed a *social* rather than a merely *personal* requirement upon morality; that according to it, morality necessarily deals with interpersonal or social conflicts of interest. This was indeed the spirit of the allocation criterion as discussed in chapter 4 and in this chapter. That moralities typically deal with matters thought to be of social importance; that social sanctions are typically advocated in support of moralities; that general, interpersonal reasons are typically thought to be required in support of moral judgments—all these features, and others, reveal the social emphasis of the allocation criterion. The refinements of the allocation criterion offered earlier in this chapter were explicitly social in import.

But this is not the only possible reply to the criticism. When we examine the reasons for including McNab's guiding principles within the pale of morality, I think we will discover that those reasons are *independent* of the fact that McNab's stoicism helps him to harmonize his personal interests with one another. McNab's stoicism is merely one of a class of codes of behavior, many of which would seem to elude the allocation criterion while counting as moralities nevertheless. I will term this class the class of codes of a *personal summum bonum*. What is characteristic of these codes is that they all offer images of a desirable or ideal life style, in some form or other; and as a class, their concern is not essentially with conflict-resolution, but with fulfilling an overriding personal ideal. Thus, whereas McNab seeks stoic equanimity, another may be captivated by a Nietzschean ideal of heroic self-affirmation—a style of life in which harmonization of interests may play no significant role.

My chief point is this: the allocation criterion, in placing emphasis upon interpersonal conflict resolution, fails to encompass a significant dimension of morality, the dimension of overriding personal ideals. Some systems of action-guiding beliefs and attitudes that deserve to be counted as moralities are concerned almost exclusively with such personal ideals. Hence the allocation criterion cannot count as a necessary mark of the moral.

In arguing that some codes of a personal *summum bonum*—codes of overriding personal ideals—count as moralities while nevertheless failing to meet the allocation criterion, I do not wish to argue that *all* such codes must count as moralities. There may be, and probably are, cases of a consuming commitment to a personal ideal or way of life which for some reason should *not* be included within the pale of morality. I shall not undertake the task of specifying the criteria that distinguish moralities from nonmoralities in this area. My purpose in this study is to show that the allocation criterion is not a necessary mark of the moral; and it is sufficient for this purpose if I have shown that at least *some* codes of a personal *summum bonum* count as moralities while failing to meet the allocation criterion.

In discussing allocation criteria of explicit appeal, I first examined a number of ways in which such criteria might vary, and suggested a series of qualifications designed to produce the version of the criterion that was most plausible and closest to the apparent intent of its defenders. I then offered a number of objections to the resulting criterion, and closed with the presentation of two putative counterexamples to the criterion, described in some detail. I believe that most authors who defend something like the allocation criterion have in mind a criterion of explicit appeal; hence my fairly lengthy attention to this kind of criterion. But criteria of objective role also have a not inconsiderable plausibility, and so we must now turn to an examination of such criteria.

Criteria of Objective Role

We must consider three main criteria of objective role: a psychological criterion, a functional criterion, and an evolutionary criterion. In the previous section I attempted to distill out of the various criteria one criterion that combined the most promising aspects of each variation. In this section, on the other hand, the alternative versions call for separate attention and separate refutation.

Regarding the psychological criterion: a person who wished to defend the allocation criterion might admit that it is possible to adhere to a recognizable morality without explicitly appealing to allocational considerations, provided that one believes in some covert, perhaps subconscious fashion that the principles to which one adheres serve allocational ends. According to such an account, the explicit defense or justification that one offers for his moral sentiments may be any of a variety of rationales, many of which can be nonallocational. What is essential in moral sentiments, it might be said, is that the person holding them somehow *feels*, in a way that he perhaps cannot verbalize, that the sentiments concern allocation issues. We may use the case of Jacoby, the sexual conservative, to illustrate the point. Jacoby objected to certain sexual practices, and defended his views on nonallocational grounds. The proponent of the psychological allocation criterion is not troubled by this fact; for, he says, we recognize Jacoby's sentiments as moral sentiments not by looking at what he says he believes, but by sensing what he *really* believes, which is that the sexual practices constitute an objectionable allocation of interest-satisfaction. It is only because Jacoby is unable to recognize the source of his own sentiments that he gives us a nonallocational defense.

The psychological version of the allocation criterion has numerous defects. The most prominent defect is that, if it were correct, we should have to be much more perceptive psychologists than we actually need to be in order to recognize moral sentiments. It is not because of our deep insight into Jacoby's true but hidden beliefs that we are able to recognize his sentiments as moral sentiments. The evidence is not some subtle psychological fact, but lies much more in the open. It has to do with what Jacoby actually says and does: his emotional condemnation of the sexual practices, his willingness to universalize his condemnation, his advocacy of severe social sanctions as penalities for the practices, his belief that the injunction against the practices is of overriding importance on the scale of value-priorities, and other related cues.

Second, if there *is* some hidden psychological ground for his sentiment, it need not be an allocational principle; the latent belief out of which Jacoby's sentiment actually springs might be a belief that God prohibits such practices, or simply that they violate sacred custom.

The case of McNab, the stoic, is even more damaging to the psychological criterion. Any attempt to find hidden allocational principles at the root of McNab's moral sentiments appears doomed to failure. McNab's devotion to psychic self-control and mastery of his emotions arises out of the value he places on the peace of mind these practices bring; to attempt to trace the practices to some hidden commitment to principles of interpersonal allocation of advantages would seem quite implausible.

It must be admitted that there is one way in which the psychological criterion offers us valuable insight. It sometimes is the case that a person's moral sentiments rest on tacit principles that he is unable to verbalize; and these principles may in some cases be allocational. Where these conditions are met, it is natural to say that the person's morality satisfies a version of the allocation criterion. But to admit this is not to give in to the allocation criterion; it is only to agree that some nonrational moralities satisfy one version of the allocation criterion. We have by no means admitted that all moralities must meet that criterion.

The second version of an allocation criterion of objective role is much more promising. I have termed it the functional criterion. The spirit of the functional criterion is roughly as follows: Granted, when people go about defending a morality, they do not always appeal to allocational considerations. People defend their moral views in a great many ways, some of which may be outlandish and irrelevant. But when we examine the function of moralities in the social structure of a group, we will find that moralities nevertheless fulfill an allocational role. They do in fact serve to adjudicate between conflicts of interests; they do in fact promote social harmony; and they are thus a necessary condition for a functioning social group. Furthermore, these are not just facts about moralities; they are partially definitive of morality. We should not call anything a morality unless we felt that it somehow actually served an allocational role in the lives of those persons who adhere to it, regardless of the explicit beliefs of those persons.

Moralities necessarily have an allocational function, and any code of behavior that strays from such a function no longer deserves to be called a morality.

Such an account has, I think, very considerable plausibility. Its plausibility arises out of several related facts. One such fact is that societies do need allocation procedures for conflicts of interest, and a morality of some kind seems to be precisely the sort of thing required to provide such procedures. Another such fact is that it is therefore plausible to suppose that moralities typically *have their origin* in the need to respond to allocation issues. Where would a society be if it had no general procedures for dealing with conflicts of interest? And what is more natural than to say that a morality is necessarily a device for providing such procedures? Hume's famous analogy of the two men in a rowboat, which asserts that morality comes into being when, in effect, men enter into a tacit arrangement to row together in order to achieve different but complementary goals, is a philosophically compelling metaphor.

But however reasonable these observations may seem, they do not require us to say that it is part of the *definition* of morality that it actually serve an allocational function. Even if we admit that moralities fit naturally into allocation contexts, I think we must also admit that a morality may achieve a kind of life of its own, and may diverge from concern with allocation issues. Furthermore, in recognizing a system of behavior as a morality, I do not believe that we are required to ascertain what actual sociological function that system of behavior fulfills. This point is especially clear when we consider not moralities as a whole, but individual moral sentiments and beliefs. When we recognize that a man has a moral sentiment of some kind, is it because we perceive what function that sentiment is actually fulfilling? The "function" of a particular moral sentiment may not even be ascertainable to us; yet we readily succeed in identifying the sentiment as moral. What are we to say when two men have directly opposing moral sentiments? Are both sentiments to have some "real function"? It would seem that we frequently encounter sentiments that are quite readily recognizable as moral sentiments, but the actual "function" or role of which is far from obvious. The distinguishing marks of a moral sentiment would seem to be independent of such a function or role.

As further support, consider the following case, which is hypothetical but not at all implausible: Specific moral directives typically presume some factual information, and this information may be false. For instance, preliterate tribes often regard it as a duty to perform certain ritualistic actions, on the (presumably) mistaken assumption that these actions will produce certain results that will constitute beneficial consequences for the members of the tribe. If, as seems possible, cases of ritualistic practices could be cited that *in fact* play no significant role in the satisfaction of human interests and in no significant way constitute an allocation of advantages, then, on the functional version of the allocation criterion, the supposed duty to perform the rituals could not count as an expression of a particular morality. Yet this is obviously an unacceptable conclusion. Moral opinions based on false information are nevertheless moral opinions; and we recognize them as such without having first to ascertain what the actual consequences may be of acting upon them. In the tribe described above, it may very well be regarded as a matter of moral significance whether one engages in the rituals or not. The associations and beliefs that accompany a practice are clearly of major importance in ascertaining whether or not it comes under what counts as a moral rule; the desideratum cannot be simply the actual function of the practice.

In fact, if we look at the actual results of various moralities, is it not possible that we will find some moralities to be actually *counterproductive* of allocational ends? Surely it is not too difficult to find actually existing moral systems which, when followed, systematically tend to *increase* social disharmony rather than to alleviate it. The functional version of the allocation criterion declares that every morality must in fact serve to resolve interpersonal conflicts of interest; by such a criterion, systematically counterproductive moralities could not count as moralities at all. And this result is surely objectionable.

Thus, although the functional version of the allocation criterion may help us to recognize a natural and appropriate role for moralities, it does not require us to say that specification of this natural role must enter into the definition of morality. Whatever their "appropriate" role, moralities may diverge from this role while still remaining moralities. In the evolution of moralities, as in biological evolution, there occur strange mutations, sports, and even monstrosities.

But perhaps we can go further. Perhaps there are some cases of moralities where it is quite *im*plausible to say that they are, as it were, offspring of some allocational parent. The case of McNab, the stoic, comes to mind. Moralities in the mode of a personal *summum bonum* would seem to have their natural home in the desire of a person to achieve a fulfilling personal life style; as such, they do not seem to fill an allocation function. The case of McNab would seem to be an especially dif-

ficult one for adherents of a functional allocation criterion.

We are left with a closely related but nevertheless distinct criterion, which I have termed the evolutionary
criterion. It does not assert that in order to identify
moralities we must always see that they now perform
some allocational function; it asserts, rather, that in
identifying moralities we must at least know that they
developed out of allocation issues. A sentiment is identifiable as a moral sentiment provided that we can at least
see that it evolved out of an attempt to deal with allocation issues—even if it now no longer has any allocational
role.

I have agreed that allocation issues provide a natural
causal origin for moralities, with the possible exception
of moralities of a personal *summum bonum*. But to specify
a natural causal origin of a thing is not necessarily to
specify a necessary condition for being that thing. The
evolutionary criterion shares many of the difficulties of
the two other criteria of objective role, and some of my
objections to the earlier criteria tell also against this one.
Just as the psychological criterion implausibly required
us to be much more perceptive psychologists than we
need to be, in order to identify moralities, so the
evolutionary criterion implausibly requires us to be
much more knowledgeable sociological historians than
we need to be in order to identify moralities. Where the
allocational role of a sentiment is not apparent to us, are
we required to make an evolutionary-historical
hypothesis that the sentiment is an outgrowth of a response to allocation issues, before we can identify the
sentiment as moral? I do not think that such a
hypothesis is logically required. The marks of a moral
sentiment, and of morality in general, are more on the

surface. They have to do with the severity of the evaluation, the willingness to universalize, the advocacy of social sanctions, and other related indicators.

But in addition to arguing that moralities may be identifiable in the absence of knowledge of their evolutionary origin, we may argue somewhat more aggressively by suggesting that a *positive* knowledge of the evolution of a morality may reveal a *non*allocational origin. Might not an inquiry into the history of a morality reveal that allocation issues did not lie at its source? A morality might, for instance, derive from the words of a prophet who was believed to be reporting the decisions of God as to what was to be permitted and what prohibited. If the words of this prophet were sufficiently revered, his pronouncements might constitute the moral law of the society, and might nevertheless be nonallocational, in function and in intention.

To appeal once more to our two test cases, Jacoby and McNab: Jacoby's sentiments regarding sexual practices were, I submit, clearly moral sentiments; yet nowhere in our account was anything said or implied about an allocational origin for his views. Jacoby's sentiments could in fact have any of several origins. One possible nonallocational origin might be that, as a child, Jacoby received religious instruction to the effect that God's revealed will prohibited the objectionable practices.

As for McNab, very little needs to be said to point out that there is no essential logical connection between an allocational origin of McNab's views, and the fact that his views constitute a morality. Neither the personal nor the social history of McNab's stoicism reveals an allocational origin that enters into identification of McNab's views as a moral code.

To sum up: the criteria of objective role that we have

examined would appear to fail as necessary marks of the moral. Neither in covert psychological feelings about morality, nor in the objective sociological function of morality, nor in the evolutionary origin of morality, can we find allocation criteria which by definition must accompany every moral code. Together with the results of the discussion of criteria of explicit appeal, these conclusions tell strongly against the claim that anything that is to count as a morality must meet some version of the allocation criterion.

But in discussing and rejecting various versions of the allocation criterion, we have omitted a consideration of what is perhaps the weakest allocation criterion of all: the *disjunction* of all of the previously considered criteria, which requires that every morality must satisfy *some one or other* of the criteria discussed above. Thus, according to this requirement, no one allocation criterion that we have examined is itself a necessary condition of every morality; but every morality must satisfy at least one of the above criteria. Loosely put, the requirement is that every morality must satisfy some allocation criterion or other from the above list, but no one in particular. Let us call such a requirement the *disjunctive allocation criterion*.

How shall we deal with the disjunctive allocation criterion? It is not correct to say that since we have refuted each of the disjuncts separately, the disjunction as a whole must therefore be false. A disjunction of non-necessary conditions of x may itself constitute a necessary condition of x. Thus, not every triangle must be scalene, and not every triangle must be isosceles, and not every triangle must be equilateral; but every triangle must be *either* scalene *or* isosceles *or* equilateral. What is needed in order to refute the disjunctive allocation criterion is some one argument or counterexample that tells equally against all of the criteria we have considered. If we review the discussion, we will find what we need. The counterexamples of Jacoby and McNab were introduced in rejecting the criterion of explicit appeal, but they were also employed in rejecting the criteria of objective role. In the face of these two counterexamples, the various allocation criteria fail; furthermore, they fail not only singly but jointly. Hence the disjunctive allocation criterion itself fails.

Concluding Assessments

If this chapter has been successful in its purpose, I have established reasonably compelling grounds for a rejection of the claim that every morality must, by definition, meet some significant version of the allocation criterion. Yet even if the reader has been convinced by these arguments, he may still feel a sense of dissatisfaction at the state of the discussion. The allocation criterion is not a necessary mark of the moral; but something like it would seem, nevertheless, to be in some significant way linked to the concept of morality. Indeed, the chief arguments of chapter 4 serve to reinforce the claim that there is some sort of intimate link between the allocation criterion and the concept of morality. If this connection is not that of necessary connection, then what is it? How are we to account for the facts adduced by chapter 4, which displayed the natural way in which allocation issues give rise to typically moral concepts, attitudes, reactions, and the like?

We have already noted that allocation issues provide at least one *very natural genesis* for morality. Wherever self-interested persons interact with one another, conflicts of interest are likely to arise, and there will be a consequent need for some procedures by which the conflicts may be harmoniously resolved in an acceptable fashion. A decent code of morality fills this need quite naturally—so naturally, in fact, that it is easy to infer that morality consists precisely and solely in the attempt to fill such a need.

But there are at least two basic flaws in such an inference. In the first place, such an account of morality overlooks the possibility of moralities in the mode of a personal *summum bonum*. To recall the case of McNab, his morality did not arise as a response to the need for allocation procedures. Second, even if one were to disallow the case of McNab, it must be said that an actually existing moral code is a practice which, once established, gains a life of its own, and thereby may drift away from its original realm of application. Though highly applicable to allocation issues, the conceptual and attitudinal machinery that constitutes a morality may become displaced onto other sorts of issues. If this displacement occurs, we may continue to recognize the phenomenon as a morality while acknowledging that it no longer concerns itself with allocation issues as such. A number of the counterexamples to the allocation criterion that I have advanced are examples where one is tempted to say that a set of moral attitudes has become *misdirected*. Jacoby, the sexual conservative, is perhaps such a case. But the crux of the matter is this: *misdirected* or *misguided* moralities are *still moralities*. Perversity invades the moral realm as well as other realms; and if the natural home of morality is in allocation contexts, we must nevertheless recognize that moralities, like other practices, may wander from their natural home, while still retaining their defining characteristics.

The sense of the previous paragraph is to suggest a claim in normative ethics: that any *acceptable* or *reasonable* morality exists as a response to the need for allocation of advantages in conflict-of-interest situations. Again setting aside the special case of codes of a personal *summum bonum*, it may be that any morality that concerns itself in no way with possible conflicts of interest, and places no value on social harmony, is an irrational and misguided morality. Many of the claims of traditional moral philosophers such as Plato, Hobbes, Locke, Hume, and others may be interpreted in this fashion. To reiterate once more: we are seeking the limits of all possible moralities, whether reasonable or misguided, acceptable or unacceptable. And if the only moralities that fail to meet some variation of the allocation criterion are misguided and unacceptable, they are moralities nevertheless.

I have suggested that a natural origin for morality may be found in the need to resolve allocation issues. I do not wish to imply that, historically speaking, this is the *only* origin of morality. Research in social anthropology reveals, I believe, other sources as well, most notably in religion, myth, and superstition. In most cultural traditions there exist precepts and prohibitions that it is natural to identify as part of the morality of the culture, but that seem to have their roots in what may be termed the prevailing metaphysics of that culture, rather than in the attempt to resolve conflicts of interest. As noted earlier in this chapter, concern for satisfaction of human interest need not be involved in such metaphysical beliefs at all.

Still, in any culture there is a compelling need for allocation procedures; and the fact remains that morality seems admirably suited to fill this need.

What, then, is the relationship between morality and allocation issues? The relationship is, I suggest, approximately the following: a) A prevailing conception of morality seems to take its character from the structure of allocation issues and the responses that are appropriate to them; b) indeed, in many cases, a given morality may be seen as an explicit attempt to deal acceptably with allocation issues; but c) moralities are complex and flexible sets of practices that may be directed to other purposes than the resolution of allocation issues, and hence d) the concept of morality is not analytically connected with the attempt to resolve allocation issues. In fact, e) although moralities appear for the most part to rest comfortably in allocation contexts, the typical machinery of morality may in some cases have its historical origin elsewhere than in allocation issues, for example in religion.

Because moralities frequently, and perhaps even typically, owe their existence to the need for allocation procedures, it is plausible to suppose that moralities by definition deal with allocation issues. But because moralities may become diverted from allocation issues or may even have other origins entirely, it is a mistake to define morality in terms of a response to allocation issues. The allocation criterion is not a necessary mark of the moral. It is not the case that all moralities necessarily concern themselves with allocation of advantages in conflict-of-interest situations.

1. W. D. Falk, "Morality, Self, and Others," in *Morality and the Language of Conduct,* ed. Castaneda and Nakhnikian (Detroit, Mich.: Wayne State University Press, 1965), p. 66.

2. In formulating the outline that immediately follows, I am heavily indebted to Professors Roderick Firth, Robert Nozick, and Charles King.

3. Although Kohlberg's Stage Five, and possibly Stage Six, are ones in which a morality is defended in terms of human welfare, his scheme recognizes as moralities codes that do not exemplify these two stages.

4. L. T. Hobhouse, *Morals in Evolution* (London: Chapman, 1951). First published in 1906.

5. Vergilius Ferm, *Encyclopedia of Morals* (New York: Philosophical Library, 1956).

6. May Edel and Abraham Edel, *Anthropology and Ethics,* rev. ed. (Cleveland, Ohio: The Press of Case Western Reserve University, 1968), p. 152.

7. Lawrence Kohlberg, "Moral Development," in *International Encyclopedia of the Social Sciences* (Macmillan and Free Press), 10: 487.

8. P. 150.

9. P. 487.

10. *Ibid.*

Bibliography

Baier, Kurt. "Moral Obligation." *American Philosophical Quarterly* 3, no. 3 (July 1966): 210-26.
———. *The Moral Point of View.* Abridged edition. New York: Random House, 1965.
Black, Max. "Definition, Presupposition and Assertion." *American Philosophers at Work.* Edited by Sidney Hook. New York: Criterion Books, 1956. Originally in Black, Max. *Problems of Analysis.* Ithaca, N.Y.: Cornell University Press, 1954.
Brosin, Henry W. "Obsessive-Compulsive Disorders." *International Encyclopedia of the Social Sciences.* Vol. 11. 1968.
Cleckley, Hervey M. "Psychopathic Personality." *International Encyclopedia of the Social Sciences.* Vol. 13. 1968.
Duncan-Jones, Austin. *Butler's Moral Philosophy.* Harmondsworth, Middlesex: Pelican, Penguin Books, 1952.
Durkheim, Emile. *Sociology and Philosophy.* Translated by D. F. Pocock. Introduction by J. G. Peristiany. Glencoe, Ill.: The Free Press, 1953.
Edel, May, and Edel, Abraham. *Anthropology and Ethics: The Quest for Moral Understanding.* Revised edition. Cleveland, Ohio: The Press of Case Western Reserve University, 1968.
Epstein, A. L. "Sanctions." *International Encyclopedia of the Social Sciences.* Vol. 14. 1968.
Falk, W. D. "Morality, Self, and Others." *Morality and the Language of Conduct.* Edited by H. N. Castaneda and G. Nakhnikian. Detroit, Mich.: Wayne State University Press, 1965.
Ferm, Vergilius, ed. *Encyclopedia of Morals.* New York: Philosophical Library, 1956.
Foote, Philippa. "Moral Arguments." *Ethics.* Edited by Judith

Thomson and Gerald Dworkin. New York: Harper and Row, 1968.

————. "Moral Beliefs." *Ethics.* Edited by Judith Thomson and Gerald Dworkin. New York: Harper and Row, 1968.

————. "When is a Principle a Moral Principle?" *Proceedings of the Aristotelian Society.* Supplementary vol. 28, *Belief and Will* (1954): 95-110.

Frankena, William K. "The Concept of Morality." *The Journal of Philosophy* 63, no. 21 (Nov. 10, 1966): 688-96.

————. *Ethics.* Foundations of Philosophy Series. Englewood Cliffs, N.J.: Prentice Hall, 1963.

————. "Recent Conceptions of Morality." *Morality and the Language of Conduct.* Edited by H. N. Castaneda and G. Nakhnikian. Detroit, Mich.: Wayne State University Press, 1965.

Gardiner, P. L. "On Assenting to a Moral Principle." *Proceedings of the Aristotelian Society,* n.s. 55 (1954-1955): 23-44.

Ginsberg, Morris. "On the Diversity of Morals." *Essays in Sociology and Social Philosophy,* vol. 1. London: William Heinemann, Ltd., 1956.

Hare, R. M. *Freedom and Reason.* Galaxy. New York: Oxford University Press, 1965.

————. *The Language of Morals.* Galaxy. New York: Oxford University Press, 1964.

Harrison, Jonathan. "When is a Principle a Moral Principle?" *Proceedings of the Aristotelian Society.* Supplementary vol. 28, *Belief and Will* (1954): 111-34.

Hart, H. L. A. *The Concept of Law.* Oxford: At the Clarendon Press, 1961.

Hartland-Swann, John. "The Moral and the Non-Moral." *Problems of Moral Philosophy.* Edited by Paul Taylor. Belmont, Calif.: Dickenson Publishing Co., Inc., 1967. Selected from, Hartland-Swann, John. *An Analysis of Morals.* London: Allen and Unwin, Ltd., 1960.

Hobhouse, Leonard T. *Morals in Evolution: A Study in Comparative Ethics,* 2 vols. London: Chapman, 1906. 7th edition with a new introduction by Morris Ginsberg, 1951.

Kluckhohn, Clyde. "Ethical Relativity: Sic et Non." *Journal of*

Philosophy 52 (Nov. 10, 1955): 663-77.

Kohlberg, Lawrence. "The Child as Moral Philosopher." *Psychology Today,* 2, no. 4 (Sept. 1968): 25-30.

————. "Moral Development." *International Encyclopedia of the Social Sciences.* vol. 10. 1968.

Ladd, John. *The Structure of a Moral Code. A Philosophical Analysis of Ethical Discourse Applied to the Ethics of the Navaho Indians.* Cambridge, Mass.: Harvard University Press, 1957.

Linton, Ralph. "Universal Ethical Principles: An Anthropological View." *Moral Principles of Action.* Edited by Ruth Nanda Anshen. New York: Harper and Bros., 1952.

MacBeath, Alexander. *Experiments in Living.* London: Macmillan and Co., Ltd., 1952.

McNeilly, F. S. "Competing Criteria." *Mind* 66 (1957): 289-307.

Mill, John Stuart. *Utilitarianism.* Library of Liberal Arts. New York: Bobbs-Merrill, 1957.

Perry, Ralph Barton. "A Definition of Morality." *Problems of Moral Philosophy.* Edited by Paul Taylor. Belmont, Calif.: Dickenson Publishing Co., Inc., 1967. Selected from Perry, Ralph Barton. *Realms of Value.* Cambridge, Mass.: Harvard University Press, 1954.

Piaget, Jean. *The Moral Judgment of the Child.* Translated by Marjorie Gabrin. Glencoe, Ill.: Free Press, 1948.

Radcliffe-Brown, A. R. "Social Sanctions." *Encyclopedia of the Social Sciences.* vol. 13. 1934.

Scriven, Michael. "The Logic of Criteria." *Journal of Philosophy* 56 (1959): 857-68.

Slote, Michael Anthony. "The Theory of Important Criteria." *Journal of Philosophy* 63 (1966): 211-24.

Sprigge, Timothy L. S. "Definition of a Moral Judgment." *Philosophy* 39 (1964): 301-22.

Strawson, P. F. "Social Morality and Individual Ideal." *Philosophy* 36 (1961): 1-17.

Toulmin, Stephen. *The Place of Reason in Ethics.* Cambridge: Cambridge University Press, 1961.

Wallace, G. and Walker, A. D. M., eds. *The Definition of Morality.* London: Methuen and Co. Ltd., 1970.

White, Morton. "A Finitistic Approach to Philosophical Theses." *The Philosophical Review* 60 (1951): 299-316.

Index